TASTE OF VENICE

TASTE OF VENICE

TRADITIONAL VENETIAN COOKING

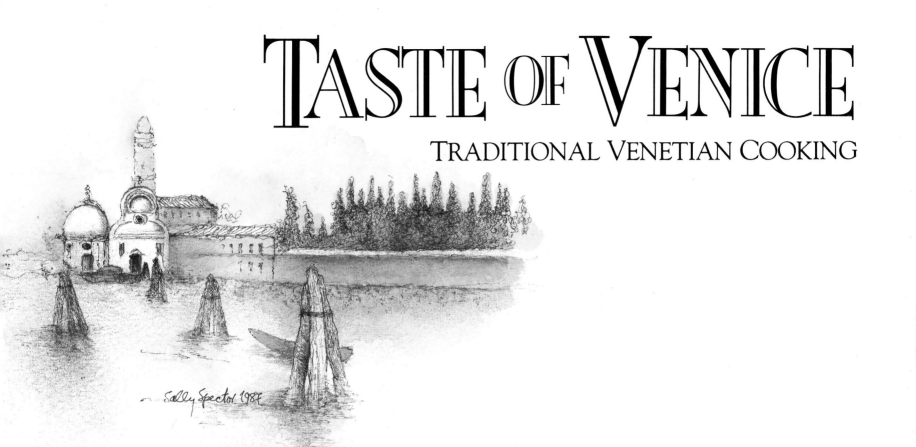

JEANETTE NANCE NORDIO

ILLUSTRATED BY SALLY SPECTOR

Salem House Publishers
Topsfield, Massachusetts

The recipe for Maffioli Sauce on page 54 is taken from *La Cucina Veneziana* by Guiseppe Maffioli (Franco Muzzio Editore).

First published in the United States by Salem House Publishers, 1988, 462 Boston Street, Topsfield, MA 01983

Created by Richard Webb and Delian Bower

Designed by Vic Giolitto

Production Nick Facer/Rob Kendrew

Library of Congress Cataloging-in-Publication Data

Nordio, Jeanette Nance, 1949-
    A taste of Venice

    1. Cookery, Italian.   2. Cookery-Italy-Venice.

    I. Title.
    TX723.N55 1988   641.5945'31   87-35764
    ISBN 0-88162-365-2

Library of Congress Catalog Card Number: 87–35764

Typeset in Great Britain by P&M Typesetting Ltd, Exeter, Devon
Printed in Italy by New Interlitho S.p.A. - Milan

CONTENTS

Acknowledgements

I wish to thank all my friends in Venice who have given moral support along the way – and it has been over a fairly long period of time! A special thanks to Nantas Salvallaggio, well known author and journalist, who encouraged me and believed in me and made me believe in 'me' too when I got bogged down. A big thank you goes to Sally Spector for consenting to illustrate this book with her lovely drawings, which capture the exact mood and subtleness of Venice, and for her helpfulness and advice, especially as she was working to a deadline. I hope we can do other books together. I thank Francesca Ellero for helping me type this 'epistle'. My thanks go to Molga Cherry Salvallaggio and Pat Western Liani for trying to find a publisher for this book in the beginning and to Lesley Ellero who read through and very helpfully corrected my errors, typing and otherwise.

My thanks also go to Mildred Taylor (whose lovely daughter is married to a smashing Venetian), who taught me her secret of making the lightest pastry, and to my Mom, Evelyn Chelleu Nance, who taught me and gave me a free hand in the kitchen when I was growing up.

Lastly I would like to thank the publishers, especially Delian Bower; also Belinda Whitworth, the editor, and Vic Giolitto, the designer.

The drawings for A *Taste of Venice* were executed in pen and ink with pencil, watercolour, coloured pencil, pastel and gouache.

6

FOR MY DAUGHTER, JESSICA, BORN A
VENETIAN OF A MERCHANT OF VENICE

JESSICA:
But love is blind, and lovers cannot see
The pretty follies that they themselves commit.

The Merchant of Venice Act II vi 37–38
WILLIAM SHAKESPEARE

Vistu che me te insegna a navegar?
Vate a far una barca o una batela;
Co ti l'a fata, butila in mar;
La te condura a Venezia bela!

(Would you like me to teach you how to sail?
Then go and build a boat or a skiff;
When you have made it, throw it into the sea;
It will carry you to beautiful Venice!)

VILLOTTE VENEZIANE

INTRODUCTION

When I first arrived in Venice, I had no idea that its cuisine would be any different from that of the rest of Italy. Quite frankly, Bolognaise sauce and the same old tomato-drenched fish and meat had begun to get quite boring, so it was a very pleasant surprise to discover other flavours and spices used to prepare delicate dishes. After my first scampi risotto, I was quite euphoric and more so when I discovered that the risotto here is made with anything that is available and in season so long as it is fresh! What a change from pasta at every meal.

My interest became even more stimulated when I discovered that you literally could not buy a Venetian cookbook in English for love nor money! So, starting with my mother-in-law and her friends and neighbours, I began collecting recipes, left, right and centre, and adapting them from the usual word-of-mouth methods, like 'a handful of this and a pinch of that'. Even the Venetians themselves didn't have a cookbook of their own, so everything was handed down from family to family. Everything had to be weighed and tested before I added it to my collection.

But my interest did not stop there; I wanted to know how and from where Venetian ingredients arrived and what dishes were eaten in past centuries. I became so involved that I was spending hours in the national libraries going through old manuscripts, books and other material, as far back as the start of the thirteenth century and in some cases even earlier. (By this time my husband, Pino, was telling me to get on with ironing his shirts!) I discovered that it was the Venetians who started the trend of cooking, still popular today, and that after the decline of the 'Serene Republic', as it was known, the great chefs left the once wealthy city and its patriarchal families to go into the service of wealthy families all over Europe, thereby influencing their eating habits.

Let me explain Venetian history a little bit to you to give you an idea where the people came from, how things developed here and how, consequently, the rest of the world was influenced.

To know a city, it is not only important to study its history, architecture, art and people, but also—to reach the very soul of the city—its cuisine and gastronomic customs. So, to have an idea of why Venetian cooking is different, you should know how certain ingredients reached and entered her kitchens. Now we should go back a bit in time.

The History of Venetian Cooking

Venice, according to one school of thought, developed in the lagoon area of the Adriatic because of people fleeing from barbarians in 451. They settled on the island known today as the Rialto area, from 'Rio Alto' as it was first known. They also settled on the islands of Torcello, Burano, now famous for its lace, and Murano, known world wide for its glassware. (There are various other islands where monasteries were founded, such as the Armenian island which today boasts the largest privately owned printing press in the world, and San Francesco del Deserto, where St Francis of Assisi sojourned.)

These people became clever seamen and cultivated the nearby islands, growing fruit and vegetables and living off the many kinds of fish and crustaceans found in the lagoon area. They learned to preserve not only meat and fish but also vegetables and fruit—a must for sailors if they are not to be plagued by scurvy.

Venice started dealing in spices early in its history. In the eleventh century the *sacchettis Venetis*—little bags of mixed spice—were sold by the Venetian traders at very high prices and were so prized that they were even left as part of inheritances. In 1204 Venice participated in the Fourth Crusade, which opened up even more areas of trade in the Near East; it then, together with Amalfi and Pisa and later Genoa, dominated commerce in the Mediterranean. After defeating Genoa in 1380 it became the most powerful seafaring and trading nation in the Occident. (Today there is an annual race still held between the four seafaring former marine republics, held in turn in each of the four places using old regatta-type boats, hundreds of years old.)

Venice's victory over Constantinople in 1204 allowed it to procure merchandise from far into that city's empire. Venice then very astutely set up warehouses at various ports to supply the rest of the Occident, and traders would send messages back and forth by pigeon post.

Venice, at that time, was dealing with Byzantines, Greeks, Hungarians, Tartars, Turks, Egyptians and Persians from whom they imported cinnamon, cloves, pepper, cassia, ginger, ambergris, sulphur, nutmeg, incense, myrrh, ivory, camphor, cardamom, indigo, benzoin and, most important of all, sugar on a large scale. Sugar was regarded as a sweet form of salt and used where salt was used! In the first cookbooks or manuscripts, most recipes, even the pasta dishes, called for sugar as one of the ingredients.

The Venetians also dealt in metals of all kinds, carpets, brocades, velvets, silks, furs, pearls and jewels of all types and, of course, perfumes. Each stone had a particular significance then, such as the agate which was said to bestow benevolence and prudence, and the pearl which was said to bring happiness (contrary to today's belief). Coral protected one from lightning, the amethyst from drunkenness, the cornelian and topaz calmed anger and the diamond rendered the wearer invisible.

The wealthy from all over the Occident came to Venice for their precious wares. You can just imagine how beautiful the Venetian women were dressed then. They were renowned for their beauty and their reddish blonde hair (obtained by lifting it on to high combs and bleaching it in the sun). The men too were well dressed and charming, with an ever ready glint in their eye to turn a coin—they haven't changed much!

You should not think of Venetians as only dealing with other seafaring nations, because they also organized overland trading. At the beginning of the ninth century Venetian traders crossed the Alps and went up the Rhine into unknown lands. They reawakened cities like Marseilles, Montpelier, Toulouse, Albi and even Paris. Cities on the Rhine like Brenner, Hamburg, Dortmund, Münster and Cologne also prospered. In 1273 Marco Polo together with his father and uncle travelled over the whole of Asia and the Far East mostly by caravan, and Marco spent seventeen years away, acting as ambassador for the Khubla Khan. When he returned to Venice he brought with him various wares, spices, textiles and articles in precious metals and he introduced what later became diffused throughout Italy—pasta.

There was already a type of pasta used but it was made differently. The pasta he introduced was called *bigoli*—a wholewheat spaghetti. It is even said that he brought Chinese cooks with him who made and demonstrated dishes to the Venetians. Today, these *bigoli* still exist and the word is also synonymous with the wholewheat type of pasta although Venetians often say *bigoli scuri* (dark *bigoli*) or *bigoli chiari* (light *bigoli* or really normal spaghetti).

Venice also dealt in salt and grains, her salt coming largely from Chioggia. In the sixth century Cassiadoro said 'Man can live without gold but cannot live without salt'. And this was certainly true of the Venetians in the beginning.

Before the Americas were discovered millet flour was used (to make polenta—a type of bread or pudding) which was inferior to the maizemeal now used. Strangely though, there are manuscripts dating back at least fifty years before the Americas were discovererd, which refer to a *yellow* polenta eaten daily in Fruili, part of the Veneto region. No one seems to know exactly where they got their maizemeal from but it seems as if it might have come via Persia.

The Spaniards introduced the kidney bean from the Americas—up until then only a type of blackeye bean had been used. It was only, too,

with the discovery of the New World and then China, that chillies and the various forms of paprika were introduced into the Venetian cuisine and eventually sold to the rest of Europe. Up to that time ginger and pepper were used to make a dish somewhat piquant.

Together with the pepper from the Mediterranean, tomato was used extensively in making sauces only in the 1700s. Onion and garlic were frequently used from very early in the eleventh century, the former finely chopped and sautéed in lard or fat till tender, the latter added after being crushed to release its juices and then sautéed till golden-brown before being discarded, as is still the habit today.

Agresto or sour, unripe grape juice or pomegranate juice was used instead of vinegar or lemon juice; the grapes were supplied by the mainlanders who cultivated grapes on a larger scale.

There is documentary proof that in the ninth century the Moslems already had culinary books and in the tenth century there are ten books listed in an Arab catalogue which were copied and printed in Venice between the twelfth and thirteenth centuries. This was done by Jambonius from Cremona who copied from the book by Gege son of Algazael, a doctor of Baghdad who died in 1100. The book contains eighty-three recipes and there is an unedited copy in Latin in Paris.

The first manuscript found on cookery in the Occident contains Occidental recipes written in the Venetian dialect of the 1400s and it is called *Libro per cuoco* (Book for the cook) and you can tell from this book in what direction the Venetian cuisine, and subsequently European cookery, would develop.

Venice, the emporium for spices, had warehouses on the Zattere, opposite the Giudecca island, filled not only with spices of every type but also with sugar. Sweet and sour dishes prevailed. (The Arabs even today have pasta pies which are sweet.) In fact, Venice tried to cultivate anything she could, but only had success with pepper, saffron, rice and sugar. Later maize was also grown. It is said that in 1334 a law was passed taxing anybody bringing sugar into the Republic of Venice because the town had started its own cultivation.

In 1475 the Duke of Milan gave the Duke of Ferrara twelve bags of rice to plant and so its cultivation spread and the Venetians dug enormous complexes of canals to cultivate this new food. Marco Polo may have brought rice from China before this and this is very possible because in *Libro per cuoco* there are a few recipes using rice and this was before the Duke of Milan's generous gesture. The Venetians with their inventiveness, with their vast amount of spices and foodstuff available, created many new risottos and *minestre de riso*. Risottos were popular because they are more warming than *bigoli* (pasta) and because rice was more readily available to the poorer people who could add practically anything (vegetables, meat and even just butter and cheese) to it.

From that cookery book and in Domenico Romoli's book in which the habits of the Venetian and Italian courts are described—printed in the 1500s—you can find the origins of the recipes which made later French cuisine so famous. We find the word *savori* or *suori* which became *saumure*—soused or pickled meat, fish or vegetables, *savore* which became *sauce*, *colla* (meaning literally 'glue' today) became *béchamel*, *patacchio* or *potaccio* became *potage*, *peverada* became *poivrade*, *papero con gli limoncelli e gli aranci* became *canard à l'orange*, *civiero* became *civiet*, *tartaresco* or *tartara* became *tartare* and so on.

In 1516 *Epulario* by Giovanni Rosselli was printed in Venice. It presented the elaborate dishes of the Venetian and Italian courts, in simple terms. This was reprinted many times up until 1750. In 1555 Jermino Ruscelli wrote (under a pseudonym) *De secreti di donno Alessio* (The secrets of master Lord Alessio), the same year, a few months later, that Nostradamus, astrologer and gastronomist of the court of France, published at Lyon a book largely 'copied' from this earlier book.

The fork was introduced to Venice in the eleventh century by the Byzantine Teodora, wife of Domenico Salvo (who was elected Doge—supreme ruler—of Venice in 1071) and daughter of the Emperor Costantino Ducas. Her *piron* (the word is still used in dialect today) or fork was made of gold and had two tines. Everywhere else in Europe and Asia at that time the custom was to use the thumb, forefinger and middle finger, as is still the custom in Moslem countries today. By the fifteenth century, the fork was firmly established at the Italian courts.

When Henry III of France visited Venice a banquet was held in his honour, and he was utterly fascinated to find that everything was made of sugar: the serviettes, knives, forks, plates and every other type of tableware. He spent the whole time crumbling the cutlery. Venice was famous for her mastery of decorating and sculpturing in sugar but unfortunately this craft has died out.

The Jewish population arrived in the twelfth century and settled on the mainland where Mestre is today. Later they moved to Venice near the state foundaries or *getti*. The name *getto* soon became *ghetto*, and this became synonymous with an area where Jewish people lived. They introduced the aubergine or eggplant which was thought to have magical qualities and also different ways of preparing vegetables which are still practised today.

Coffee was imported from the Turks in 1640 as a medicine, but when the Venetians discovered that if sugar was added to it, it was much nicer tasting, it became popular as a drink on its own. In 1683, Venice opened up the first coffee shop in St Mark's Square—the square known today as the 'drawing room of Europe'.

The arrival of Napoleon and the battle of Merengo, after which his personal chef created the dish of chicken and tomato sauce, heralded change for the Venetians, because Napoleon sold Venice to the Austrians. The Austrians sent an army of Croats, Slavs, Austrians and Czechoslovakians, the majority German speaking. These were, after a while, absorbed as Venetians as they became bilingual, and naturally they also added their touch to the cuisine of today: *goulasch*, their form of the original Venetian *carne pastissada*, still in use today, *kraphen* and *chifel*, which are pastries eaten for breakfast; potatoes; and Prague ham (cooked ham slightly smoked). After a brave stand against the Austrians, Venice finally joined the rest of the states of Italy in 1866 to form the Republic of Italy.

Essential Notes on Using the Recipes

Venetians have managed to retain their unique traditions, feasts and public holidays, mostly dating back centuries, and this is because of their great pride in their unusual city and its history. Because of the importance of these feast days there is a list of them at the end of the book, describing what happens and what special food is eaten. You can then find the recipes for this special food within the book.

All the recipes are for *four* people unless otherwise stated. Details of oven temperatures used are given in the Conversion Charts. In case you need any help locating some of the ingredients, there is a Glossary with the Latin names of some of the fish and a list of UK/US word equivalents—but most should be easily available. Sopressa is a Venetian sausage and maizena is a fine cornflour like arrowroot or potato flour. White wine vinegar is used unless otherwise stated and *fresh* herbs are always used. Two varieties of paprika are used, sweet and hot or piquant, and tomato purée (not to be confused with tomato concentrate) is made with fresh or tinned tomatoes, chopped extremely finely.

All the recipe names are given in Venetian dialect or old Venetian, and all the recipes which appear with precise dates have come from my researches into ancient cookbooks and manuscripts. These recipes have been adapted and tested by myself and many have been used as part of an antique Venetian menu they served at the Cipriani Hotel in Venice. I hope you enjoy trying out these and all the other Venetian recipes in the book for yourself.

1 APERITIVI

APERITIFS

The most common aperitif is a glass of white wine nicknamed here in Venice – but nowhere else in Italy – an 'ombra' or 'shadow'. This goes back to the end of the fourteenth century when there were wine stalls with tables around the campanile in St Mark's square and these tables were continually moved around the square following the shadow which was cast by the campanile in the heightening and setting sun. The people of Venice would go off to have their 'ombra' out of the broiling sun. The saying originally was 'to go drink in the shadow' but over the centuries it has become to go drink an 'ombra'.

Spritz Liscio
Spritzer

Half a glass of dry white wine topped up with soda water.

Spritz con Bitter
Spritzer with Bitter Campari

Half a glass of dry white wine and a half-tot measure of bitter Campari topped up with soda water.

Spritz con Select
Spritzer with Select

Select is a low-alcohol drink, similar to Campari but more orange in colour.
    Half a glass of dry white wine and a half-tot measure of Select topped up with soda water.

Bellini
Fresh Peach Juice Cocktail

Purée fresh depipped and peeled peaches in a liquidizer adding a drop of lemon juice so that the liquid keeps its colour and a little sugar to taste if so desired. Alternatively, if you are fortunate to find bottled peach juice (even the type sold for babies), you may use this.
    Half fill a glass with the peach juice and top up with sparkling white wine.

Mimosa
Fresh Orange Juice Cocktail

Half a glass of freshly squeezed orange juice topped up with sparkling white wine.

Tiziano
Titian Cocktail

Blend in a food processor or liquidizer washed sweet black grapes (the very small type) – these are called 'fragola' or 'strawberry' grapes here. Pass through a muslin cloth, twisting the cloth. The juice will be quite clear.
    Half fill a glass with the grape juice and top up with sparkling white wine.

Americano
Americano

¾ dry Vermouth, ¼ bitter Campari and a piece of lemon peel (zest), topped up with soda water.

Ponte de le Do Spade

2 ANTIPASTI

HORS D'OEUVRES

In any Venetian restaurant the most frequently found *antipasto* – and the most typical – is an *antipasto de pesse*. This consists of various types of fish and crustaceans – whatever is available at the time – preboiled, allowed to cool and then dressed with oil and vinegar or lemon, chopped parsley and bruised garlic. The latter is only used for its flavour, usually not eaten. The mixture is left to marinate for a few hours before serving.

The second most common and most typical *antipasto*, to be found not only in Venice but in the whole of Italy, is a large plate of assorted cold cuts such as various types of salami, hams (cooked, smoked, Parma), very thinly sliced roast beef and pork. This is also served with hardboiled eggs, halved and dressed with oil, vinegar, salt and pepper. Pickled vegetables may also be served with this.

The following *antipasti* can also be eaten as a main course, in which case the quantities should be doubled; the vegetable *antipasti* can be used as a side dish.

Cuor de Articioco
Artichoke Hearts in Olive Oil

Hearts look like small roses. The outer tough leaves are peeled away.

24 small globe artichokes
½ cup lemon juice
3 cups dry white wine
2 tblspns vinegar
3 bayleaves
3 cloves garlic, bruised
4 tblspns finely chopped parsley
olive oil, as required
3 cloves garlic, bruised
seasoning to taste

Remove outer leaves and tops of artichokes. Cut off excess stalk. Dip them into lemon juice to prevent browning. Mix together in a pan wine, bayleaves and garlic, add artichokes and simmer for 10 minutes or till artichokes are tender. Drain artichokes thoroughly and place in a dish. Cover with a good amount of olive oil, the vinegar, garlic cloves and parsley and seasoning to taste. Every now and then, turn them over to ensure that they absorb the dressing.

This will keep for a long time if stored in a closed jar.

OSTERIA

14

Osteria

Fondi de Articioco a la Veneta
Artichoke Fonds Veneta

Fonds are the flat bases.

8 large globe artichokes
3 tblspns finely chopped parsley
3 cloves garlic, bruised
approx ½ cup olive oil
seasoning to taste

Fonds can be bought prepared and ready for cooking. However, all one needs to prepare them oneself is a sharp knife. Peel the artichoke all around the bottom as one would an apple. Cut the stem off the bottom so that it is flat on the bottom, cut the leaves off the top, leaving a piece of base about ½in/1cm high (keep leaves and stems to make artichoke soup).

Place the bases in salted boiling water and gently simmer till tender. Place in a serving dish and while still hot cover with olive oil, garlic, parsley and seasoning. Allow to cool before serving.

These will keep for 3–4 days, covered, in a refrigerator.

Cavial del Po
Po Caviar

History recounts that in the past the Po was so abundant with sturgeon that they could be easily caught and in enormous numbers. The French under Napoleon, during their invasion, denuded the woods along its banks and pushed mud into its waters, creating a muddy river. The sturgeon could not survive under those conditions and so they are not as abundant as in the past. The roe of the Po fish is considered to be more 'tender' and delicate than the Russian type.

sturgeon roe or caviar
oil (preferably olive)
fresh brown or French bread

Mix the caviar with a little oil and place in a dish under crushed ice. Spread on the bread to eat.

This is usually served with a chilled white wine or sparkling wine.

Granceole
Crab

1 large crab
juice of ½ lemon
olive oil
seasoning to taste
½ tblspn finely chopped parsley

Place the crab in boiled, fresh, cold water till it loses consciousness, then place it in salted boiling water and cook for 10 minutes. Remove from the water. Drain right side up. Remove the underside flap, legs and roe. Carefully remove all the white flesh and coral and finely chop these together. Add the other listed ingredients to the finely chopped flesh and mix well to amalgamate. Allow to marinade for 15 minutes.

Carefully clean the crab shell, removing any viscera, put the crab flesh mixture into the shell and garnish with parsley.

Fondi de Articioco in Forno col Pien
Artichoke Fonds Stuffed and Baked in the Oven

8 large globe artichokes
2 hardboiled eggs
2 slices of smoked or cooked ham
2 tblspns finely chopped parsley
1 tblspn finely chopped basil
salt and pepper
olive oil
breadcrumbs

Prepare the artichoke bases as described in the second recipe in this section. Place in boiling salted water and cook till almost tender (10 minutes). Allow to cool. Finely chop or mince or blend together the egg, ham, parsley and basil. Add salt and pepper to taste. Place the cooled artichoke bases in a buttered ovenproof dish and put some of this stuffing mixture on each artichoke, pressing it down slightly. Sprinkle each with breadcrumbs and then put a little oil on each. Bake in a moderate oven until breadcrumbs are golden-brown. Serve hot or cold.

A little grated hard cheese may be added to the stuffing mixture.

As an alternative to using fonds, open small artichokes like a flower and remove choke.

Bovoleti
Snails

These are also eaten as snacks with wine.

Small snails, found in gardens and farms preferably where lettuce is cultivated, are used. Place them in a large bowl of fresh water in order that they may lose their viscidity. Remove them from the bowl and wash them under a tap of running cold water. Place them in a pot of cold water and heat. Remove them as soon as a foam appears on the surface.

1lb 2oz/½kg small snails in their shells
olive oil
3 tblspns finely chopped parsley
3 garlic cloves, finely chopped
salt and pepper

Once the snails have been removed from the pot and drained, mix all the other ingredients together and pour over the snails. Mix the dressing and snails well so as to ensure that the dressing is absorbed by the cooked snails. Serve cold or warm with plenty of French bread.

Tinned snails may also be used for this recipe.

Melon e Parsuto
Cantaloup Melon and San Daniele or Parma Ham

San Daniele ham comes from nearby Udine and is deliciously sweet and salty. (A Jewish custom here is to serve the melon with truffled eggplant – see under Vegetable section, *Melanzane Trifolate* – instead of the ham.)

1 large cantaloup divided into 8 segments
12 very thinly sliced pieces of San Daniele or Parma ham

Remove sweet flesh of the melon from each segment and cut into 4 pieces or leave as 'gondolas'. For each serving arrange 2 segments or equivalent pieces on a small plate and arrange 3 pieces of ham around these.

Each piece of melon is eaten with a piece of ham. A knife and fork is used.

Ostreghe a la Venessiana
Venetian Oysters

16 oysters, scrubbed
4 tspns caviar
½ tspn pepper, cayenne pepper or hot paprika

Open oysters keeping both shells. Mix together the caviar, pepper and lemon juice and spread thinly over the oyster. Close shell and serve on ice. Serve with brown bread and butter.

bianco e
rosso sfuso   350
prosecco   700
Fragolino   800
Malvasia   700

Sally Spector 1987

Osteria

Ostreghe a la Marie-Hélène
Oysters Marie-Hélène

16 oysters, scrubbed
1 medium onion, finely chopped
½ cup vinegar
black pepper

Open oysters taking care not to spill any of the 'juice'. Mix the onion, vinegar and pepper; serve in a gravy boat. The oysters are eaten on toasted brown bread and butter with a good helping of the sauce.

Pomodori col Pien de Ton
Tomatoes with Tuna Stuffing

4 medium tomatoes
1 small tin tuna (light meat)
1 small onion, grated
2 tblspns mayonnaise
paprika (hot)
salt to taste

Remove a 'lid' from the top of each tomato, put aside and scoop out tomato flesh with a teaspoon. Flake drained tuna and combine with onion, mayonnaise, paprika, chopped flesh from tomato and salt, if required. Mix well and use to fill the tomato cups. Replace the lid.

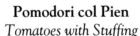

Pomodori col Pien
Tomatoes with Stuffing

These are delicious hot or cold. Sopressa is a Veneto salami. The aubergine stuffings in Chapter 6 can also be used.

4 medium tomatoes
2 pieces of sliced salami or sopressa, minced
2 slices of ham, minced
2 eggs, beaten
1 tblspn chopped parsley
breadcrumbs to bind
4 tblspns oil
salt and pepper
1 clove finely chopped garlic
3 tblspns finely grated Parmesan or hard cheese

Halve the tomatoes and place in a buttered ovenproof dish. Mix all the ingredients together well, adding enough breadcrumbs to form a not too moist stuffing. Put about a dessertspoon of this mixture on each of the halves pressing down slightly to flatten. Dot with a little oil and bake in moderate oven till the tomatoes are tender and the stuffing is golden-brown.

Peoci e Peverasse in Salsa
Mussels and Clams in Sauce

A mixture of clams and mussels can be used, or just mussels, or instead of small clams, cockles may be used.

2lb 3oz/1kg mussels (clams, cockles)
4 tblspns cooking oil
2 cloves of garlic, bruised
3 tblspns of finely chopped parsley
1 tblspn lemon juice (optional)
pepper (and salt to taste, if necessary)

Under cold water scrub and clean mussels with a sharp knife, removing beard. Rinse under running water to remove any sand or grit. Discard any broken or open mussels.

In a large wide pan heat the oil and put the garlic and lemon juice in the pan together with the mussels (still in their shells). Stir the mussels around and cover pan with lid. Cook for about 10 minutes until they open. Discard any that are not open, first trying to reheat them, in case they did not get enough heat.

Remove mussels from pan and place in a large shallow ovenproof dish. Add the rest of the ingredients to the 'sauce' in the pan. Pour this sauce over the mussels and serve with crusty bread.

This dish is usually placed in the middle of the table and each person has a plate which is used to discard the mussel shells. The hands are used entirely and the bread is used to mop up the delicious sauce made by the mussels. A definite must for this dish is extra large serviettes!

(This dish may also be served as a main course but the quantities must be increased.)

Scala Bovolo

Peoci col Pien
Stuffed Mussels

2lb 3oz/1kg mussels
2 tblspns finely chopped parsley
1 cup fresh breadcrumbs
2 cloves garlic, finely minced or chopped
salt and pepper
3 tblspns grated Parmesan or hard cheese
2 tblspns oil

Clean and cook mussels as above. Remove from pan and remove empty half of each shell. Place full mussel halves in large, shallow, ovenproof dish, so that each shell touches the other. Mix the parsley, breadcrumbs, garlic, salt, and pepper, cheese and oil together. Put a little of this mixture on each mussel and press down slightly. If mixture is too dry (this depends on freshness of breadcrumbs) add a little more oil. Bake in a moderate oven till golden-brown.

Fasioi Bianchi
Butter Beans

In the 'osterie' or pub-type bars these are served on small side plates per person with toothpicks to pick the beans up from the plate, and with a glass of wine.

9oz/¼kg (prepared weight) dried, fresh or tinned butter beans
1 onion, finely chopped
1 clove garlic, sliced
salt and pepper
oil and vinegar

Soak dried beans in water overnight. Place in large pot with fresh unsalted water (do not ever cook these in salted water as they will remain hard) and bring to boil. When the beans are just starting to boil a foam will appear; drain the beans and put into pot again with fresh water and bring once again to the boil. Cook till almost tender *then* add a bit of salt to the water. The beans are done when they are tender right through but are not too tender that they break up – one could almost say, like when cooking pasta, that they should be '*al dente*'.

Drain beans and put into a serving bowl and add the onion, garlic, salt, pepper, oil and vinegar to taste. Mix well and stir every now and then to ensure that the beans absorb the dressing.

If you use fresh beans these do not need to be soaked but should be cooked as the dried beans. Tinned beans just need to be drained and then dressed.

These can also be served as a side dish.

Fasioi Borlotti e Ton
Red Kidney Beans and Tuna

9oz/¼kg (prepared weight) dried, fresh or tinned red kidney beans
1 medium-sized onion, finely chopped
2 cloves of garlic, bruised
3 tblspns olive oil
salt and pepper
2 tblspns lemon juice
8oz/225g tin tuna fish
1 tblspn chopped parsley

Prepare the dried, fresh or tinned kidney beans as the butter bean recipe above.

Mix together the oil, lemon juice, onion, garlic and seasoning. Add the beans and parsley and chill.

Flake the tuna into fairly good bite-size chunks and mix into the beans just before serving.

Venetian Lagoon.

S'ciosi al Forno a la Venessiana
Venetian Baked Snails

24 large snails, fresh or tinned

for stock:
Water, salt, carrot, thyme, celery, garlic and bayleaf

for stuffing:
2oz/50g butter
3 tblspns finely chopped parsley
3 tblspns garlic cloves, finely chopped or minced
seasoning to taste

If using fresh snails, put them (in shells) in a pot of boiling water which contains a good handful of wood ash. Leave to boil for 25 minutes. Remove from pot and drain and with a needle remove from shells.

Now proceed with fresh or tinned snails as follows. Prepare the stock and when hot put the snails in it, so that the flesh will absorb all the various flavours. Boil the snails for 15 minutes. Drain and leave to dry.

Clean and dry the shells thoroughly. Put a little of the stuffing which has been thoroughly mixed together at the bottom of each shell and replace a snail in each shell, sealing the mouth of the shell with a little of the stuffing. Place the snails in an ovenproof dish and bake in the oven for 15 minutes at about 350°F/180°C.

These are eaten with a toothpick.

S'ciosi in Salsa
Snails in a Sauce

24 large snails, fresh or tinned
2oz/50g butter
1 tblspn flour
1 cup white wine
1 small onion, grated
seasoning to taste

Prepare the snails as in paragraph one of the previous recipe.

Prepare the sauce by melting the butter in a pot and adding the flour and mixing well to make a roux. Add the wine, salt, pepper and finely grated onion. Stir till smooth but not too thick. Serve in a separate bowl.

Each snail is removed with a toothpick and dipped into the sauce.

Garusoli o Caragoi
Seasnails or Whelks

In either of the above two recipes, seasnails or whelks can be used instead of snails.

Cape Sante a la Venessiana
Venetian Scallops

12 large scallops
breadcrumbs
5–6 tblspns oil
1 clove garlic, bruised
1 tblspn parsley, minced or finely chopped
2 tblspns white wine or lemon juice
seasoning to taste

Open the scallops by prizing them with a sharp instrument; remove the mollusc, debeard and remove the intestine. Wash mollusc well and roll it in the breadcrumbs.

In a pan put the oil together with the garlic and parsley and heat. Sauté the garlic and parsley till garlic becomes golden-brown. Remove garlic and discard. Add the scallops to oil and sauté these till golden. Add the wine or lemon and simmer for a few minutes, stirring well.

Distribute scallops with their sauce on to 4 of the concave shells.

Fighi col Parsuto
Fresh Figs with San Daniele or Parma Ham

8 fresh figs
16 pieces very thinly sliced San Daniele or Parma ham

Peel and halve the figs and wrap a slice of ham around each half, or quarter the figs and cut each slice of ham in half and wrap around a fig quarter. Spear with a toothpick.
Place each serving on a well-washed fig leaf.

Brasaela col Pompelmo e Rucola
Brasaela with Grapefruit and Rucola

Brasaela is a cured dried beef and rucola (rocket) is a sharp salad leaf.

12 thin slices of brasaela
2 grapefruit, peeled with all white pith removed, and divided into segments
2 handfuls of salad leaves, the small type if rucola not available

On four small plates place three slices of brasaela in the centre, then in a circle around it place the grapefruit segments. Then in a circle around the grapefruit arrange the rucola.

Houses and Canal

3 MINESTRE

Soups, Risottos, Pasta, Polenta and Gnocchi

Soups, risottos (rice dishes), gnocchi (potato dumplings – pronounced 'nokki') and pasta are all types of first course traditional in the Veneto area and above all its capital, Venice.

Soups

Broeto a la Ciosota
Chioggia Fish Consommé

This is a seventeenth-century recipe, still in use.

1lb 10oz/750g fish trimmings
2lb 3oz/1kg firm-flesh fish, scaled
6 shrimps, shelled
6 mussels, without shell and with beards removed
1–2 cloves bruised garlic, according to taste
salt and pepper to taste
2 tblspns olive oil
1 tblspn vinegar
1 slice lemon
2 peeled tomatoes

Wash the scaled fish.

Place oil in ceramic or enamel pot – never metal – and heat. Add the garlic and sauté till golden-brown. Remove the garlic.

Boil the fish trimmings separately in a generous amount of water.

Add the firm-flesh fish, shrimps and mussels to the oil and turn regularly till coated with oil and then add the boiled fish trimmings, vinegar, tomatoes and lemon. Simmer together for about 15 minutes. Remove the lemon. Strain mixture, stirring well so as to press out all the pulp and flesh. Return to the pot and add the seasoning. Add more water to the pot (about 2 cups per person).

Serve with croutons or fresh French bread.

Sopa de Pesse
Fish Soup

This is different from the consommé, because it is served with fish in pieces and with the shrimps whole and mussels in their shells. Madame Stravinsky, wife of Igor Stravinsky who is buried in Venice, said before she died that if money was unlimited, she would have had the *sopa de pesse* from the famous Harry's Bar in Venice flown out every Friday to the States where she lived.

2lb 3oz/1kg firm-flesh fish, scaled and cut into pieces
1lb 10oz/750g fish trimmings
8 medium shrimps, unpeeled
16 mussels cleaned and without beards, in shells
1 medium-sized onion, sliced and chopped finely
2 stalks of celery, chopped
2 tblspns butter
2 tblspns olive oil
1–2 cloves garlic, bruised
4 large tomatoes, peeled *or* 6 tblspns tomato sauce
(*see* Sauces)
1 tblspn finely chopped or minced parsley
salt and pepper to taste

Wash and clean the fish. Place oil and butter in pot and sauté onion and garlic till browned. Remove garlic. Place fish, fish trimmings, unpeeled shrimps and celery in this pot and cover generously with water. Add salt and pepper. Simmer for about 10 minutes. Remove the fish and shrimps and put to one side. Shell the shrimps and put with fish. Replace shrimp shells in pot. Let the pot simmer for another 20 minutes.

Strain this mixture, stirring well so as to press out all the pulp and flesh, then pour a little boiling water over the remains to get as much flavour out as possible. Add more water if not enough to allow 2 cups per person.

Put the liquid back on the heat and add the fish, shrimps, mussels in their shells, chopped

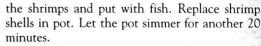

tomatoes and parsley. Season to taste. Simmer
for 10 minutes or until the mussels have opened.
Discard any which do not open after this time.

Serve in deep bowls, with equal amounts of
the various types of fish and shellfish per person
arranged around the sides of the bowls. Toast
some rounds of French bread and arrange these
around the edges of the bowls as well.

Chioggia

25

Sopa de Castra
Mutton or Lamb Soup

1lb 10oz/750g lean mutton or lamb
4 cups of water
1 medium carrot
2 large stalks of celery, chopped
1 medium onion, chopped
4 large potatoes, quartered
salt and pepper
grated Parmesan or grana padana cheese

Cube the meat, removing all fat. Wash the meat, place it in a pot and cover with cold water. Bring to the boil, skimming off all the scum that appears. Add all the rest of the ingredients except the potatoes and cheese. Cover the pot with a well fitting lid and simmer till tender.

When the meat is quite tender, add the potatoes and simmer until these are cooked but still firm. Add a little more water if the consistency is too thick or if there is not sufficient to allow 2 cups per person. Adjust seasoning.

Serve sprinkled with the grated cheese.

Tripa Coada
Casseroled Tripe Soup

Coada means a soup cooked at a very low heat.

1lb 2oz/½kg tripe, cleaned and chopped into largish pieces
3½ oz/100g margarine or fat
3 carrots, chopped
2 tblspns chopped or minced parsley
2 bayleaves
generous pinch of thyme
2 cloves
1 clove garlic, bruised
1 cup white wine
enough stock to cover
grated Parmesan or grana padana cheese

Place a layer of some of the carrots and parsley on the bottom of a large and deep pot dotted with the margarine or fat. Place a layer of the tripe on top. Repeat this process until all the ingredients are used. Add the stock, wine and spices, herbs and garlic. Dot with some more fat. Cover and place in a low oven for 4–5 hours or until the tripe is tender.

Sprinkle the cheese on each serving.

Sopa d' Intingolo
Stewed Mushroom and Giblet Soup

This is a recipe from the 1600s, still in use.

1lb 2oz/½kg chicken giblets, finely chopped
1 onion, chopped
2–3 tblspns dried or fresh mushrooms, sliced (if dried, soak in water till plumped out)
2 stalks celery, chopped
1 large carrot, diced
3 tblspns butter
1 cup white wine
8 cups (minimum) beef stock
salt and pepper to taste
grated Parmesan cheese

Sauté the onion, mushrooms, celery and carrot in the butter till nicely browned and tender. Add the giblets and brown for 2–3 minutes. Add stock, wine and seasoning. Simmer for ½ an hour.

Serve each portion with a sprinkling of cheese.

Sopa de Cape
Clam or Cockle Soup

3lb 5oz/1½kg baby clams or cockles or any mixture of this type of shellfish
3 tblspns cooking oil
1 clove garlic, bruised
2 tblspns finely chopped or minced parsley
1 large cup beef stock, hotted up
1 cup water
salt and pepper to taste

Wash and scrub the shellfish well. Heat the oil in a fryingpan which has a well-fitting lid. Add the garlic and parsley and sauté till the garlic is a light brown then remove the garlic and discard. Add the cup of water and season to taste.

Heat this all up till hot and add the shellfish. Put lid on pan and gently shake the pan keeping over the heat. Look from time to time to see if all the clams have opened. *Discard any which have not opened.* Add the cup of hot beef stock.

Serve in a long, flattish dish with fresh French bread to sop up the juices. This is usually eaten communally from the one dish but may be served individually. This may also be served as a main course.

Squasseto a la Bechera in Minestra
Butcher's Stewed-meat Soup

This is a recipe from the 1700s, still in use.

7oz/200g chopped lungs
1lb 2oz/500g oxtail, in pieces
7oz/200g tripe, chopped
1 onion, chopped
1 carrot, diced
1 stalk celery, chopped
2 tblspns fresh thyme in a gauze bag or bouquet garni
salt and pepper to taste
approx 8 cups water
grated Parmesan cheese

Place the lungs, oxtail and tripe in a pot of boiling water and boil for 5 minutes. After this time throw away the water and put the meat back into the pot with fresh water, salt and pepper to taste, celery, carrot and onion and a bag of thyme or bouquet garni and simmer gently till the meat is tender and the liquid is reduced. This is rather a watery soup.

Serve with a piece of toasted bread on the bottom of each soup plate and pour soup over this. Serve with grated cheese.

Pan Onto o Pan Bogio o 'Sopa da Gati'
Oily Bread or Boiled Bread or 'Cat's Soup'

This a porridge-like soup which is very tasty and is made with leftover bread. It is usually made for old people or young children. For children omit the herbs and salt and add sugar. This recipe is falling into disuse.

53fl oz/1½ litres water
1 clove garlic, bruised
1 small piece fresh rosemary
1 Salvia (sage) leaf
1 tblspn olive oil or butter
grated cheese

Boil the bread in the water, add the salt and herbs and stir constantly till it cannot be stirred any longer and has become a thick porridge. Serve with the butter or oil and a good serving of grated cheese.

Archangel Gabriel
Palazzo Ducale

from Capella Corner
FRARI Church

from Church of SanSimone Grande

15th century Venetian sculpture
Salla Spector 1987

from Capella Corner
FRARI Church

from the tomb of l'Ubertino da Carrara
Church of the Eremitani, Padua

Angels
15th century Venetian sculpture.

Sopa de Cavei de Anzelo
Angel's Hair Soup

8 cups or more of beef stock
3½oz/100g very fine hair-like pasta
salt and pepper to taste
a pinch of nutmeg
grated Parmesan cheese

Bring stock to the boil and add the nutmeg and seasoning to taste. Add the pasta and stir over heat until the pasta is cooked. Serve with a generous sprinkling of Parmesan cheese.

Kitchen of the 18th century

Risottos

Mention Italy and without fail the mental picture conjured up (and due mostly to the film industry) is of a swarthy man in his undershirt or vest at a kitchen table with a steaming bowl of spaghetti in front of him! However, unlike south and central Italy where pasta is the most important first course – and not necessarily eaten as described above, in the north rice plays the most important role as a first course.

Venice has always been famous for its risottos (spelt *risoti* in the Venetian dialect) and *minestre de riso* with fish, more than any other first course. In fact there are so many ways in which rice may be prepared that one might well ask what cannot be used to make a *minestra de riso* or a risotto. The wonderful *minestre de riso* which have the appearance of velvet softness even though they are soupy in texture and the risottos which have a creamy, pasty appearance but in which every grain of rice is separate and *al dente* (firm), can be made with practically anything one can find in the cupboard or fridge – no matter how bare these might be!

There are many types of rice to be found in Italy today, such as *originario*, *arborio*, *maratello vialone* and *vialone nano*. They do have one thing in common and that is that they are mostly a short, roundish grain, opaque in the centre and transparent around the edges. When cooked properly and *al dente* – 'to the tooth' which means not too hard but not too soft – the rice grain *just* loses its hardness in the centre and becomes opaque all over. (The exact timing for cooking a risotto or a *minestra de riso* is not possible to give with any great accuracy as this depends on the rice type but it is more or less twenty minutes of almost constant stirring. Depending on how 'soupy' the dish is, most of the liquid will be absorbed and the rice should not be strained.) Do not despair if this small type of rice is not available where you live; the normal long-grain rice will suffice even though it's not exactly right and you will have to use more of the basic sauce to get the right texture to the final dish.

Rice was known to exist during the times of the ancient Greeks and Romans and was later introduced by the Arabs to the Spaniards and then to Italy, becoming popular in the Middle Ages and especially popular in the north of Italy with its abundance of rivers along the banks of which to cultivate it. Why does it now play such an important role in Venice compared to the rest of Italy? The answer might well be psychological, but it's probably more feasible that it's because of the humidity and gloominess of the winter climate: rice is easy to store and, cooked in the traditional Venetian manner, it retains its heat thus heating the organism, giving one a sense of well-being and, literally, warming the 'cockles of the heart'.

As in other countries where a hearty, steaming bowl of thick soup is the custom in winter, the Venetians have their *minestre* and risottos and, I might add, that today this does not only apply to winter. A Venetian would rather forego the second course than give up his *minestra* or risotto! Goldoni, the famous Venetian playwright of the 1700s, demonstrates the importance of rice to the Venetians in his comedy *Sior Tódoro Brontolon* (Mr Theodore the Complainer). That comical but very avaricious personality describes how its possible to feed eight or nine people with a small amount of rice! He tells the maid to put the rice on to boil early in the morning. When she enquires if he will be eating earlier than usual, he replies that he will be lunching at the usual time but if one puts the rice on early one can virtually see it increasing before one's eyes. (Rice, the more it's cooked, the more it swells, which gives the impression that more has been used. Naturally the texture and consistency would be like soggy pudding!)

Risi e Bisi
Rice and Peas

This is one of the most famous rice dishes from Venice. It can be made with fresh, frozen or tinned peas, and is a good example of a dish which can be prepared, no matter how bare the cupboard!

The famous Italian composer, Rossini, while living in Venice and sitting in his favourite *osteria* (pub-restaurant), the Salvadago, near St Mark's Square, wrote the '*Risi*' Chorus in his opera *Tancredi* while waiting for his *risi e bisi*. Also in the same *osteria* while impatiently waiting for his meal and getting quite annoyed at the waiter who continuously ignored him, he apparently picked up his fork and started tapping his glass in front of him in order to attract the waiter's attention. As he was doing so, his musical ear picked out a melody and so his *La Semiramide* was born!

This was the traditional dish eaten by the Doge of Venice on St Mark's Day, 25 April. It's still as traditional today in Venice as is *pasta e fagioli* (pasta and beans).

35fl oz/1 litre stock
1 clove garlic, bruised
1 onion, roughly chopped
10½oz/300g fresh *or* frozen peas *or* 1 large tin peas
1 good handful fresh parsley, finely chopped or minced
2oz/50g butter
16 heaped tblspns of Italian short grain rice
a pinch of nutmeg
a dash of brandy (optional)
salt and pepper to taste
grated Parmesan cheese
2oz/50g bacon, cubed

Sauté the onion and garlic in the butter till the garlic turns a light golden-brown. Remove garlic and discard. Add the peas and sauté these till tender, adding a little stock from time to time to prevent them sticking. Add the nutmeg, parsley, the rest of stock and bacon and simmer for 3 minutes. Add the rice and stir constantly while keeping the rice just off the boil. (Rice dishes must be constantly stirred or else they stick.) Add a little more boiling water or stock (which has been kept hot in another pot on the stove) from time to time while stirring to keep the rice moist but not too soupy.

When cooked *al dente* (see explanation at the beginning of chapter) – this will take about 20 minutes – add the seasoning, if required, the dash of brandy and the cheese and stir a few times to allow the alcohol in the brandy to cook away. This is a *minestra* and should have a slightly liquid texture.

Serve in soup plates with a dot of butter on top and a generous sprinkling of cheese.

Risi in Cavroman
Rice with Lamb

The name 'Cavroman' is indicative of the Levantine influence as a result of the many voyages made by the fleet of the Venetian Republic to the Orient. Note also the use of the cinnamon.

16 tblspns rice
1 onion, chopped
10½oz/300g shoulder or back mutton or lamb, not too lean, cut into cubes
2oz/50g butter
3 peeled, seeded and chopped tomatoes
2 small pieces of cinnamon
1 litre of stock
½ cup white or red wine
grated Parmesan cheese
seasoning

Sauté the onions in the butter and when tender add the lamb. Brown the lamb all over and add the tomatoes and cinnamon. Simmer all this on a low heat for 2 hours adding stock from time to time to prevent drying out. When cooked and quite tender add the rice and more stock and stir till the rice is cooked (about 20 minutes). Adjust seasoning.

Serve immediately with a dab of butter and some grated cheese.

Carrack - 15th century ship

Risi e Luganeghe
Rice and Sausages

Luganeghe are pork sausages which are very fatty and the pork is minced rather on the coarse side. Preboil, changing water twice, to remove excess fat, if desired.

16 tblspns rice
3–4 pork sausages, skinned and chopped
35 fl oz/1 litre (approx) stock made
from beef and chicken
2 oz/50 g butter
1 onion, chopped
1 clove garlic, bruised
grated cheese
seasoning

Sauté the onion and garlic in the butter until the garlic is light brown. Remove and discard. Sauté the chopped sausages together with the onion till cooked but not crisp. Add some boiling stock to this and then the rice. The stock must just cover the rice. Proceed as for '*Risi e Bisi*', stirring constantly and adding stock from time to time. Adjust seasoning.

Serve when *al dente* (about 20 minutes) with a dab of butter and the grated cheese.

Risi in Cagnon
Rice with Butter and Cheese

No one knows where the name in Venetian dialect comes from or what it means. Another 'Old Mother Hubbard' recipe.

16 tblspns rice
35 fl oz/1 litre plus of chicken stock
5oz/150g butter, diced into fairly large pieces
grated Parmesan cheese
seasoning

Cook the rice in the stock, adding seasoning to taste, till *al dente* (approximately 20 minutes of stirring and cooking). Remove pan from the heat and place rice mixture in a large bowl. With a wooden spoon mix in the pieces of butter, added one at a time to the rice, slowly stirring till the butter is melted and incorporated into the rice. Adjust seasoning.

Serve with a very generous sprinkling of cheese.

Garden of the Abbey of the Misericordia

Risi coi Fenoci
Rice with Fennel

1 tblspn parsley, finely chopped or minced
6 small and tender fennel roots, diced
2oz/50g butter
a little oil
1 onion, chopped
3 rashers bacon, diced
35 fl oz/1 litre (approx) chicken stock
16 tblspns rice
grated cheese
seasoning

Sauté the onion in the butter and oil and, when almost tender add the fennel roots and sauté these until also tender and slightly golden in colour. Add the bacon and parsley. Add a little stock from time to time and simmer gently for about ½ hour. About 20 minutes before serving, add the rice to this sauce and cook for about 20 minutes, stirring. An extra spoonful of butter may be added while stirring. Adjust seasoning.

Serve immediately with a dab of butter and some grated cheese.

In exactly the same way as this recipe, substituting the fennel, one can make:

Risi e Ponte de Sparesi
Rice and Asparagus Tips

1lb 2oz/½kg fresh asparagus tips boiled in salted water till tender *or* 1 large tin of asparagus tips

Risi e Bruscandoli
Rice and Wild Asparagus

1lb 2oz/½kg wild asparagus (*luppola* or hops) boiled in salted water till tender

Risi e Suchete
Rice and Courgettes

1lb 2oz/½kg diced courgettes

33

Risi e Suca
Rice and Pumpkin

12oz/350g pumpkin (not the watery or stringy kind),
boiled till tender
pinch of cinnamon

Risi e Tegoline
Rice and Green String Beans

1lb 2oz/½kg beans, cleaned and chopped

Risi e Coste de Rapa
Rice and Beetgreens

1lb 2oz/½kg beetgreens, boiled till tender in very little
water – use water with stock for extra flavour

Risi e Spinassi
Rice and Spinach

1lb 2oz/½kg spinach, boiled till tender in very little
water or stock

Risi e Cavolfior
Rice and Cauliflower

1 small cauliflower, chopped and boiled till tender in
salted water

Risi e Sedano
Rice and Celery

6 stalks of celery, chopped

Risi e Parsemolo
Rice and Parsley

instead of the 2 tblspns parsley use 2 cups of finely
chopped parsley and plenty of cheese

Risi e Salate o Radiccio Rosso
Rice and Salad Leaves or Red Radicchio

use all the outer green leaves of a lettuce (preferably
romaine), chopped (keep heart for salad)
if using radicchio, chop and use all of it

Risi e Sepoline
Rice and Small Cuttlefish

1 clove garlic, bruised
2 tblspns finely chopped or minced parsley
1 tblspn oil
2 tblspns butter
8 small cuttlefish, cleaned and chopped (remove ink,
eyes, mouth and shell)
1 cup white wine
water or stock
16 heaped tblspns rice
seasoning to taste

Sauté the garlic till golden-brown in the butter
and oil. Remove garlic and discard. Add the
cuttlefish and wine and simmer till liquid has
almost cooked away. Add the rice and water or
stock – enough just to cover the rice. Stir
constantly adding water or stock a little at a time
till the rice is *al dente* (about 20 minutes). Add
parsley in last 10 minutes. Check seasoning.
Serve immediately.
   Although with fish risottos cheese is not
usually served, most families add a little to
amalgamate all the ingredients while the rice is
cooking.

Risi e Bisato
Rice and Eel

1 eel, skinned and cut into pieces
1 clove garlic, bruised
1 tblspn finely chopped or minced parsley
1 tblspn oil
2 tblspns butter
1–2 drops lemon juice
1 bayleaf
water or stock (chicken or light beef)
grated cheese (optional)
seasoning to taste

Sauté garlic in oil and butter till golden-brown.
Remove and discard. Add eel, bayleaf and lemon
juice and simmer gently. When eel is almost
cooked add the rice and a little of the stock.
Cook rice for about 20 minutes adding a little
stock at a time and stirring constantly. Add the
parsley in the last ten minutes. Adjust seasoning.

When rice is *al dente* serve immediately, with a
little cheese if desired.

Risoto con le Patate
Potato Risotto

This is quite delicious, even though rice with
potatoes sounds odd.

3 thick rashers of bacon, diced
1 large onion, chopped finely
1 sprig fresh rosemary
4 large potatoes *or* 6 small to medium ones, peeled and
cut into small pieces
chicken or beef stock
seasoning to taste
grated cheese

Sauté onion, rosemary and bacon in butter and
oil till onion is tender and slightly golden and
the bacon not too crisp. Add the potatoes and
leave them to braise with the onion and so on till
they are golden in colour. Add rice and stock as
before and proceed in the same manner. Adjust
seasoning.
   Serve hot with grated cheese.

Risoto alla Chioggiotta (o de Go)
Chioggia (Goby) Risotto

A very typical dish which utilizes these lagoon or canal fish, or rock fish as we know them. The skin is removed before straining as this would make the sauce grey.

1½ lb/700g goby, washed in water and vinegar with heads and insides removed
2 cloves garlic, bruised
14oz/400g Italian rice
seasoning to taste
1 dssrtspn butter
2 tblspns white wine
2 tblspns grated cheese
water or stock if necessary
seasoning

Bring the goby to the boil in 35fl oz/1 litre of water and boil for about 15 minutes. Remove the skin and strain the liquid and flesh through a fine strainer, pressing well to strain through all the stock and flesh. Season to taste. Place in a pot and bring to the boil.

Add the wine, garlic and rice and cook, stirring from time to time and adding a little water or chicken or fish stock if necessary as this risotto must be on the liquidy side. Adjust seasoning.

When the rice is *al dente*, add the butter and cheese. By adding the last the risotto becomes less liquid and more creamy.

Risoto co la Ua
Grape Risotto

1 clove garlic, bruised
1 tblspn oil
2 tblspns butter
1 large bunch (approx 1lb 2oz/½kg) of black,
Malaga-type grapes
16 heaped tblspns rice
2 tblspns finely chopped or minced parsley
grated cheese
seasoning to taste
chicken stock

Sauté the garlic in the butter and oil till the garlic is golden-brown. Remove and discard. Add the grapes and cook gently for 5 minutes. Add the rice and the stock and proceed as before. Check seasoning. Add the parsley 10 minutes before the end. Serve with a generous sprinkling of cheese.

Risoto a la Bechera
Butcher's Risotto

3 tblspns butter
a little oil
1 onion, finely chopped
1 carrot, finely chopped
1 celery stalk, finely chopped
1 tblspn tomato sauce (see Sauces)
or 2 tblspns peeled and chopped tinned tomatoes
7oz/200g of mixed leftover meat or offcuts (soup-meat
diced, chicken giblets diced, etc)
7oz/200g veal, cut into small pieces
beef stock
seasoning
16 heaped tblspns rice
grated cheese

Sauté the onion, carrot and celery till tender in the butter and oil. Add the beef and brown nicely, then add veal and other meat or giblets and tomato and simmer for 20 minutes. Check seasoning. Add the stock and rice and cook as before for about 20 minutes, stirring. Serve hot with cheese.

Risoto co le Secole
Spinal Meat Risotto

This recipe uses the meat and fat which covers the vertebra and which is extremely tasty.

7oz/200g spinal meat, diced
2 large onions, finely chopped
3 tblspns butter
1 tblspn tomato sauce (see Sauces)
or 2 tblspns of peeled and chopped tinned tomatoes
a pinch of cinnamon
seasoning
a piece of beef soup-meat
beef stock
grated cheese

Sauté the onion in butter till tender. Add the spinal meat, soup-meat, tomato, cinnamon and about 1 or 2 tblspns of the stock. Simmer for about 2 hours till tender. Add rice and more stock and cook as before till the rice is *al dente*.
Serve with grated cheese.

Risoto de Sepe col Nero
Cuttlefish and Ink Risotto

This sounds awful and to some probably looks awful too but is *very* tasty with a much stronger taste of fish. It can also be made without the rice, with 1lb 12oz/800g cuttlefish cooked till tender and the sauce fairly thick. This is known as 'Cuttlefish with very Black Sauce' or '*Sepe col Tocio Nerissimo*'.
Bigoli (wholewheat spaghetti) or ordinary spaghetti may be served with this as sauce (omitting rice).

8 cuttlefish, cleaned and sliced (with inksacs removed
and one kept aside) and the eyes, mouth and hard
parts removed
1 large onion, chopped
1 clove garlic, bruised
3 tblspns butter
1 cup white wine
16 heaped tblspns rice water
1 tblspn oil

Sauté the onion and garlic in the butter till garlic is golden-brown. Remove garlic and discard.

Add the cuttlefish and inksac and wine and just cover with water. Put a well fitting lid on pot and simmer gently till tender.

Remove the pieces of cuttlefish from the sauce and put aside (if allowed to cook with rice these would become very tough from over-cooking). Return the pot to the heat and when the sauce begins to boil, put in the rice and cook as all previous risottos, adding a little water at a time.

A few minutes before the rice is ready, add the cuttlefish and stir for a few minutes. This dish does *not* need salt.

Risoto de Sepe senza Nero
Cuttlefish Risotto without Ink

This is made exactly as the above recipe, but without the inksac. At the end add seasoning, and adjust to taste.

Palazzo Ducale

Campo San Giacomo - Rialto Market

Risoto de Fongi
Mushroom Risotto

These mushrooms may be the dried type soaked in tepid water to plump them out or any fresh type.

16 heaped tblspns rice
5oz/150g sliced mushrooms
1 large onion, chopped
3 tblspns butter
1 tblspn parsley, finely chopped or minced
1 garlic clove, bruised
1 cup white wine
2 tblspns tomato sauce (*see* Sauces)
or 4 tblspns of peeled and chopped tinned tomatoes
stock
grated cheese (optional)
seasoning

Sauté the onion and the garlic in the butter till garlic is golden-brown. Remove and discard garlic. Add the mushrooms and parsley and sauté for a few minutes. Add the wine and simmer till the wine has been reduced. Add the rice, tomato sauce and stock and cook rice as previously explained. Season to taste.

Serve with a sprinkling of grated cheese and a dab of butter if desired.

Risoto col Safaran
Saffron Risotto

1 large onion, finely chopped
1 garlic clove, bruised
1 tblspn parsley, finely chopped or minced
1 cup mushrooms, sliced and sautéed in butter
10½oz/300g of chicken livers or leftover mixed meat
½ tspn/3g saffron
1 tblspn brandy
2 tblspns butter
stock
pinch of nutmeg
16 heaped tblspns rice
seasoning

Sauté the onion and garlic in the butter, removing and discarding the garlic once it becomes a golden-brown colour. Add the meat and sauté this too until browned. Add the

mushrooms, nutmeg, saffron and brandy and a little stock. Simmer for ½ hour or until the meat is tender.

Add the rice, parsley and stock and proceed as before in previous recipes. Season to taste.

Serve with sprinkling of cheese.

Risoto de Peoci o Vongole
Mussel or Clam Risotto

2 tblspns oil
2lb 3oz/1kg mussels or clams, cleaned, scrubbed and debearded
1 onion, finely chopped
1 tblspn parsley, finely chopped or minced
2 tblspns butter
seasoning to taste
16 heaped tblspns rice

Place the cleaned clams or mussels in a pan with the oil and about 2 cups of water. Put this on to heat and bring to boil with lid on pan.

When the mussels or clams have opened, remove the flesh from the shells. *Throw away any which have not opened at this stage.* Reserve the liquid.

Sauté the onion in the butter and add the clams or mussels, parsley and juice in the pan. Add the rice and cook as for previous risotto dishes. Adjust seasoning. Serve hot.

As I have said before, rice dishes with fish are not served with cheese but one can add a little at the end of the cooking process to amalgamate the ingredients.

Risoto de Gamberi o de Scampi o Ragosta o Granseola o Coa de Rospo o Oltro Pesse
Shrimp, Scampi, Lobster, Crab, Monkfish (Angler Fish) or any other Type of Fish Risotto

7oz/200g shellfish, shelled, or fish, deboned
and filleted
1 onion, finely chopped
1 tblspn tomato sauce (*see* Sauces)
or 2 tblspns of tinned tomatoes, peeled and chopped
(optional)
1 tblspn parsley, finely chopped or minced
1 cup white wine
4 lemon wedges
seasoning
3 tblspns butter
16 heaped tblspns rice
grated cheese (optional)

Sauté the onion in half the butter till tender adding a little water so it remains white and does not become golden in colour.

Add the tomato if required and fish and sauté these for a few minutes. Add the wine and parsley and simmer for 3 minutes. Add the rice and cook as previously explained. Season to taste.

Add the rest of the butter and serve with a wedge of lemon and if desired (but not traditional) a very small sprinkling of cheese.

Risoto a la Pilota
Rice-husker's Risotto

As can be seen from the name, this is a recipe which was invented by rice-huskers or *piloti*. These huskers work in the paddies.

14oz/400g rice
35fl oz/1 litre (approx) hot stock
2oz/50g butter
½ onion, finely diced
4 small pork sausages (salamelle), skinned and diced
grated Parmesan cheese or similar
1–2 tablespns olive oil

Grease a casserole dish with the oil and pour the rice slowly into the dish so that it forms a conical shape. Add enough stock to cover the rice ½in/1cm from the top of the cone.

Bring to boil and allow to boil quite furiously for about 5 minutes stirring all the time. Then cover with well fitting lid to prevent the stock from evaporating and reduce the heat to minimum and cook till *al dente* without stirring again.

In the meantime, melt the butter and sauté the onion till slightly golden.

Add the skinned and not too finely chopped pork sausages (salamelle) and allow to cook gently so that they lose their excess fat but do not become crispy. Add the rice and cheese and mix well.

Instead of the sausages, some minced sirloin of pork may be used, but then increase the amount of butter.

Pasta

Naturally not everyone makes their own pasta any more because of all the bought varieties now available, but it does make a change as the taste is really different.

For each recipe I've listed the type (shape) of pasta usually used in Venice for that particular sauce but any pasta may be used.

Pasta co Agio e Ogio
Pasta with Garlic and Oil

This is a recipe from the 1500s, still in use.

14oz/400g spaghetti
1 clove garlic, finely chopped
1 tblspn parsley, finely chopped
5–6 tblspns olive oil
Parmesan cheese
seasoning to taste
a little butter (optional)

Bring a pot of salted water to the boil and put the spaghetti in it, turning it in slowly till it softens so it can be cooked without breaking. Stir occasionally so that it does not stick to the bottom of the pot.

Meanwhile, mix the rest of the ingredients except the cheese in a pot and heat a little.

When the spaghetti is *al dente* (cooked through but firm – about 8 minutes) drain well and put back into the pot. Pour the sauce over and add the cheese, mixing thoroughly. Add a little butter if so wished. Serve immediately.

Pasta co Agio e Ogio e Peperoncino
Pasta with Garlic and Oil and Chillis

This is made in exactly the same way as above but with the addition of small dried chillis. On average, for four people, three small dried chillis are used finely chopped, but this depends on how hot you like the dish.

Bigoli in Salsa
Wholewheat Spaghetti in Anchovy Sauce

This is a recipe from the 1400s, still made today in the traditional way.

14oz/400g spaghetti
10½oz/300g salted sardines or anchovies
(tinned variety may be used)
4 onions, finely chopped and boiled till tender
2 tblspns fresh cooking oil

Bring a pot of salted water to the boil and add the spaghetti without breaking it. Stir occasionally to avoid it sticking at the bottom of the pot.

Meanwhile, thoroughly wash the sardines or anchovies in fresh water to remove excess salt and chop them.

Place them in a pan together with the drained onions and oil and simmer together till well blended and almost creamy.

When the spaghetti is *al dente* drain and place in a large bowl. Add the sauce and mix together thoroughly so that the pasta is well coated with the sauce. Serve immediately.

Campo del Milion

Pasta e Fasioi
Pasta and Beans

This is one of the most traditional and popular pasta dishes in Venice. The kidney beans (red) usually used are *borlotti* or *lamon*. While once this dish was poor man's fare (noble families not letting on that they too enjoyed it in privacy), today it is enjoyed by all, not only because of the flavour but because the lowly bean of yesteryear has risen in price and is no longer a 'cheap' meal!

10½oz/300g kidney beans
1 tblspn oil
1 onion, chopped
1 clove garlic, peeled and crushed
1 finger-length sprig of fresh rosemary
1 carrot
1 stalk celery
1 stock cube
pinch of cinnamon
seasoning to taste
1 potato
1½oz/40g bacon or spek
3½oz/100g pork sausage or piece of pork
7oz/200g pasta (*subiotini* or *tagliatelle*)

41

Soak the dried beans overnight in water with a pinch of bicarbonate of soda added to the water. (This softens them more than normal.) Next morning when nicely plumped out, rinse them thoroughly in fresh water.

In a large soup pot place the beans, onion, carrot, celery, garlic, potato, rosemary (stalk removed and leaves finely chopped or minced), bacon and sausage and cover with water. Cook till the beans are tender but not broken. Remove half the beans together with the carrot, onion, celery, garlic and potato, and 'mouli', mince or put into a blender till the consistency of a thick creamy sauce. Put back with rest of ingredients. Add stock cube, cinnamon and seasoning to taste. Add more water if too thick. Heat and add the pasta. Cook till pasta is *al dente*.

The end result must be thicker than a cream soup. Correct seasoning once more and add the olive oil.

Spaghetti coe Vongole
Spaghetti with Cockles or Baby Clams

This dish can be made with the baby clams in their shells, and the dish then becomes a finger bowl affair (*see below*)!

14oz/400g spaghetti or *bigoli* (wholewheat spaghetti)
2lb 3oz/1kg baby clams in their shells
or 1lb 2oz/½kg shelled (fresh, canned or frozen)
6 tblspns olive oil
2 garlic cloves, peeled and bruised
4 tblspns tomato sauce (*see* Sauces) *or* 4 large peeled and chopped tomatoes
1 tblspn finely chopped parsley
seasoning to taste

Wash and scrub the clams thoroughly, especially if serving them in their shells.

Heat 1 tblspn oil in a pan with a lid, place the clams in the pan and cover. Gently shake the pan over the heat till the clams have opened, *discarding any which have remained closed*. Remove clams and strain juice and put both to one side.

Remove the clams from their shells if serving shelled. Add the 5 tblspns of olive oil to a small pot and heat. Add the garlic and sauté till golden-brown, remove and discard. Add the

tomato, clam juice, and seasoning, and cook for about 30 minutes. Add the clams and cook gently for a minute or two. If sauce seems too thick add a little water. Add the parsley.

Bring a pot of salted water to the boil and add the spaghetti. When *al dente*, drain and place in a large bowl. Mix thoroughly with the sauce. Serve immediately.

If, as I mentioned, the clams are served in their shells, allow a finger bowl of warm water and lemon per person.

Spaghetti o Pasta coi Peoci
Spaghetti or Pasta with Mussels

This is made in exactly the same way as the recipe for cockles and clams except mussels are used and these are thoroughly scrubbed clean, debearded and removed from their shells.

Spaghetti col Ton
Spaghetti with Tuna

1 large tin of tuna in (olive) oil
1 large onion, finely chopped
1 clove garlic, peeled and bruised
3 tblspns tomato sauce (*see* Sauces) *or* 4 peeled and chopped tomatoes *or* the tomatoes may be substituted by a 'white' sauce
1 tblspn finely chopped parsley
2 tblspns olive oil
seasoning to taste
14oz/400g spaghetti or any other pasta
a little hot paprika (optional)
a little cheese (optional)

Heat the oil and gently sauté the garlic and onion till tender and the garlic golden-brown. Remove the latter and discard. Add the tomato, if using, parsley, the tuna, finely flaked, and the seasoning to taste. Cook for a further 3–4 minutes. If sauce seems too dry add a little more olive oil or a little butter.

Meanwhile, cook the pasta till *al dente* and drain. Pour into a large bowl and thoroughly mix with sauce till each piece of pasta is coated.

Many families include a little cheese with this dish, although this is not traditional.

Pasta ala Rabiata
Pasta with a Hot (Angry) Sauce

14oz/400g *penne* (short macaroni)
1 onion, finely chopped
1 aubergine, finely chopped
1 large bell pepper (red or green), diced
2 small dried chillis, finely chopped
4–6 tblspns olive oil
seasoning to taste
grated Parmesan cheese
2 cloves garlic, peeled and bruised
2 large tomatoes, peeled and chopped

Heat the oil and sauté together onion, aubergine, pepper, tomatoes and garlic. Remove garlic and add seasoning to taste, together with the chillis. Simmer for 3 minutes till all ingredients are tender and the sauce is thickish.

Cook the pasta as described in previous recipes, and serve with the sauce and a helping of grated cheese.

Windows on a Canal

Sally Spector 1987

Spaghetti a la Marinara
Sailor's Spaghetti

Who knows why this is so called, as there is not a bit of fish in this recipe. Perhaps because the fishermen could not stand the taste of fish after a while or perhaps this was invented on one of their 'bad-luck' days!

14oz/400g spaghetti or *bigoli* (wholewheat spaghetti)
3 cloves garlic, peeled and bruised
4 tblspns olive oil
4 cups tomatoes, peeled and chopped
1 tblspn parsley, finely chopped
½ tspn basil
1 pinch oregano
seasoning to taste
3 tblspns tomato sauce (*see* Sauces)
or 1 of tomato concentrate
grated Parmesan cheese

Heat oil, add garlic, tomatoes, parsley, basil and seasoning and cook for 20 minutes. Remove garlic. Add the oregano and tomato sauce or concentrate and cook till mixture thickens – about 15 minutes.

Bring a pot of salted water to the boil and cook spaghetti till *al dente*. Drain.

Serve with sauce on each serving and a generous sprinkling of grated cheese.

Spaghetti coi Figadini
Spaghetti with Chicken Livers

14oz/400g spaghetti or *bigoli* (wholewheat spaghetti)
2 tblspns olive oil
1 onion, finely chopped
1 cup tomato sauce or peeled chopped tomatoes
4oz/100g mushrooms, sliced
14oz/400g chicken livers, chopped
seasoning to taste
grated Parmesan cheese

Heat the olive oil in a pan and sauté onion till tender and slightly golden in colour. Add the chicken livers, mushrooms and seasoning. Sauté the chicken livers till cooked through but

tender. Add the tomato and simmer for a further 10 minutes.

Cook spaghetti as per the previous recipes and pour sauce over.

Serve with grated cheese.

Pasta consa coi Bisi
Pasta with a Pea Sauce

14oz/400g spaghetti or other pasta (eg *tagliatelle* or *penne*)
1 onion, chopped
5oz/150g ham, finely diced
1 large tin peas *or* 2 cups fresh or frozen peas
3 tblspns butter
½ cup thin cream
a dash of brandy (optional)
seasoning
grated Parmesan cheese

Sauté the onion in the butter till tender. Add the ham and peas and simmer with a little water or juice from tin for about 20 minutes till the peas are tender. Add the cream and brandy and cook for 5 minutes. If the sauce becomes too thick after adding the cream, add a little stock. Add seasoning to taste.

Cook the pasta as per the previous recipes and serve with the sauce and a generous serving of grated cheese.

Pastizzo de Pesse
Fish Lasagne

This dish is also called 'alla Buranella'. The velouté fish sauce may also be used with *tagliatelle* made with eggs.

35fl oz/1 litre of fish sauce made as the '*Broeto a la Ciosota*' at the beginning of this chapter (do not sieve the clams and mussels) – shrimps may be added too
2 cups of cheese, grated
lasagne pasta – preferably egg pasta
1oz/30g butter
¾oz/20g maizena *or* 1½oz/40g flour
9fl oz/¼ litre milk

Melt the butter and stir in the maizena or flour, as one would to make a white sauce. Add the fish sauce, together with the clams and mussels and shrimps. Make a creamy sauce, not too thick, of coating consistency.

Cook the lasagne as directed by manufacturer or, if using fresh, or pasta which does not need precooking, use as is. (If using lasagne pieces which do not need precooking, it is important to remember that the béchamel or velouté sauce

Fondamenta Rossa

must be liquidy and not thick, as the pasta absorbs liquid while cooking.) In a rectangular or square dish, place a little of the sauce at the bottom then a layer of pasta, a layer of sauce and a sprinkling of cheese; repeat this till all the ingredients have been used, ending with the sauce and a generous sprinkling of cheese.

Bake in oven at 400°F/200°C till golden on top (about 30–45 minutes) and the pasta is cooked through.

Pastizzo de Macaroni
Macaroni Pie

for the pastry:
7oz/200g flour
3½oz/100g butter
2oz/50g sugar
1 egg

7oz/200g macaroni
1 cup breadcrumbs
1 cups grated cheese
14oz/400g chicken giblets, chopped
4oz/100g mushrooms, chopped
2 small stalks celery
2 smallish carrots, chopped
if available, a few pieces of boiled pigeon (optional)
26fl oz/¾ litre stock
seasoning to taste
1 egg, beaten, for brushing on to pastry

Mix all the listed pastry ingredients together to form a firm pastry. Roll out into two large disks, one to fit the bottom of a round pie dish and the other slightly larger for the top.

Precook the macaroni and drain.

Place the stock in a pot and add the giblets,

celery, carrots, mushrooms and pigeon. Simmer till tender and there is a fairly thick sauce. Season to taste.

Place the smaller round of pastry in the pie dish, sprinkle with breadcrumbs and place a layer of macaroni, then ragout, and then cheese, repeating till all these three are used up. Cover with the second piece of pastry and seal the edges. Brush with beaten egg and bake in oven at 400°F/200°C till pastry is cooked and golden.

Pastizzo de Melanzane
Aubergine Pie

The layers of this and the next two pies can also be interspersed with lasagne.

2 large aubergines (*see* 4 medium)
9oz/250g mozzarella, thinly sliced
35fl oz/1 litre tomato sauce (*see* Sauces)
2 cups grated cheese (preferably Parmesan)
flour
cooking oil (for frying)

Slice the aubergines lengthwise thinly or into thin rounds. Salt and leave to drain with a weighted-down plate on top. (Place the slices preferably at an angle so the excess water can drain off.)

Leave for 1 hour and then pat dry with paper towels. Dip in milk and then coat with flour and gently sauté in hot oil till golden-brown. Drain on paper towels.

Butter a casserole dish and line the bottom with aubergine slices, then a layer of tomato sauce, and then a layer of mozzarella cheese, and a little Parmesan. Repeat these layers, ending with the mozzarella, till all the ingredients are used up.

Bake at 400°F/200°C for 15 minutes or until golden on top.

Pastizzo de Suchini
Courgette Pie

Proceed as per the aubergine pie, using 6 large courgettes.

Pastizzo de Articiochi
Artichoke Pie

3 cups of tomato sauce or peeled chopped tomatoes
7oz/200g artichoke hearts, thinly sliced
flour
2 eggs, beaten
1 cup oil
1 litre of béchamel sauce
seasoning to taste
1 cup (approx) grated Parmesan cheese

Coat the artichoke slices in flour and dip into beaten egg. Sauté gently in oil till golden. Remove and drain on paper towel.

Grease a casserole dish and place a layer of artichoke, then a layer of tomato, then a layer of béchamel and then a sprinkling of the grated cheese; repeat, ending with a layer of béchamel and cheese.

Bake in oven at 400°F/200°C for a ½ hour or until golden-brown on top.

Polenta and Gnocchi

Polenta is very popular in the north of Italy and especially in Venice where it accompanies most of the traditional dishes. It can be made with the yellow or white maizemeal.

Gnocchi, or dumplings as many have translated the word, are also very popular in Venice and as traditional in all their various types as risottos. I cannot stress here the importance of using *old* potatoes if making potato gnocchi. New potatoes are too watery and absorb too much flour and the gnocchi tend to break up while simmering in the water or they have a very doughy taste. Another tip is to boil the potatoes in their jackets because it definitely improves the flavour, be it for gnocchi or for mashed potatoes – or as we say here 'creamed' potatoes.

Canal Grande : Deposito del Megio and Fondago dei Turchi

RIO DEL
MEGIO

Polenta

35fl oz/1 litre water
1 heaped tspn/7g (approx) salt
10½oz/300g maizemeal
53fl oz/1½ litres water, kept hot in separate pot

Bring the 35fl oz/1 litre of water to the boil with salt added. Add the maizemeal to the water by gradually sprinkling it into the water and stirring all the time. This prevents lumps from forming. *Always stir to the right* – Venetians swear by this! Stirring all the time and always to the right, when the meal gets hard add a ladleful of hot water. This is basically the secret of a good polenta – hardening it over the heat and softening it with the water.

After about 15 minutes one could say that the polenta is done but not for the Venetians. They carry on with the cooking and this makes the maizemeal more digestible. After a ½ hour the polenta becomes the right consistency and starts coming away cleanly from the sides of the pot. One could stop here too, but the Venetians continue the cooking for another ½ hour, stirring all the time, always to the right.

A good polenta cooked this way has an unmistakable texture and taste and is easily digested.

After an hour remove the polenta from the heat and pour it on to a large wooden board. Large round ones are sold in Venice especially for this purpose. The polenta is never cut with a metal knife, but with a piece of string or a wooden knife.

Polenta may be eaten on its own with butter and/or cheese or with any other dish as a substitute for bread.

It is also very good grilled on a barbecue or heavy-bottomed grill pan. It should be well grilled so that it forms a crust and can be lifted and turned, but do not leave it so long that it burns.

Pastizzo de Polenta
Maizemeal Pie

polenta, as made in previous recipe, and allowed to cool
35fl oz/1 litre meat sauce or leftover stew with a little stock added to make a thick sauce
1lb 2oz/500g mushrooms, sliced and sautéed in 2 tblspns butter and 2 tblspns water
2 cups Parmesan cheese, grated
4oz/100g butter, diced

Cut polenta into layers, each about a finger thick.

Butter a baking dish about 8 × 10in/20 × 25cm and place a piece of polenta on the bottom, cutting it to fit. Then put a layer of the meat sauce, a layer of mushrooms dotted with butter, some cheese. Repeat these layers till all the ingredients have been used, ending with polenta. Dot last layer of polenta with butter and bake in an oven at 375°F/190°C for ½–¾ hour till golden-brown.

Gnocchi de Patate
Potato Dumplings

It is essential that *old* potatoes are used as new potatoes are too watery and absorb too much flour. A useful tip is to wait till the potatoes are tepid and then add the flour. This is *not* one hundred per cent correct and traditional and many people frown at it, but the gnocchi will definitely have more of a potato flavour.

4lb 6oz/2kg old potatoes
14oz/400g flour (this is approximate as it depends on the quality of the potatoes)
2 eggs
salt

Scrub and wash the potatoes well. Boil them in their skins till tender and then remove the skins while still hot. (A clean, folded tea towel helps to prevent burnt fingers!) Mash the potatoes well. Add the flour and knead the mixture till well blended.

Add the eggs and mix and knead once more, till it becomes a firm, rollable dough, adding more flour if needed.

Flour a table top. Divide the mixture into 4 parts. Roll each part into a long roll, finger thick. Cut at an angle every 1in/3cm or so.

Take a curved grater and flour the back of the grater. Roll a piece of the dough down the back of the floured grater with the middle finger. The gnocchi will have tiny indentations on the outside from the grater and one large indentation on the inside where the middle finger pressed into it as it was rolled downwards to the bottom of the grater. They will be oval and curved in shape. This is the traditional shape but not to worry if this does not come right. Instead roll out a little thinner and cut into cubes.

Bring a pot of salted water to the boil and add the gnocchi one at a time and not too many for the pot as they will stick to each other. When they rise to the surface leave for a minute or so longer and remove with a perforated ladle.

Serve each portion immediately it is removed from the water, or keep warm, till all are cooked, in a bain-marie system with a tblspn of butter.

Gnocchi may be served with any type of sauce but the most commonly used are butter and cheese, tomato sauce or meat sauce. The latter is very often the sauce from the stew which is to be served as the second course.

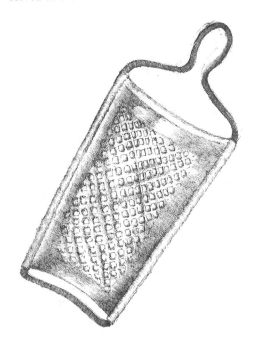

Gnocchi de Pan e Luganega
Bread and Sausage Dumplings

2 eggs
3 pork sausages, skinned
2 tblspns Parmesan cheese, grated
7oz/200g flour
butter and cheese for serving
14oz/400g old bread, soaked in water
and squeezed out till crumbly
3 tblspns flour

Mix all the ingredients except the flour and blend together till a paste. Put the flour on a table top in a mound. Wet hands. Take a spoonful of the mixture and, removing from the spoon, roll it in the flour till well coated. Repeat till all the mixture is used.

Put gnocchi into simmering water one at a time and not too many at a time in the pot. Remove after they have risen to the surface as in recipe before and keep warm.

Serve with a pat of butter and grated cheese.

Gnocchi de Semolin
Semolina Dumplings

8 cups stock
2 eggs, lightly beaten
4oz/100g semolina
1oz/30g butter
pinch of nutmeg
3 tblspns finely chopped parsley
Parmesan cheese, grated

Melt the butter slowly in a double boiler. Remove from the heat and add the egg, a little at a time, mixing it in well, then add the rest of the ingredients. This should form a fairly thick mixture.

Bring the stock to the boil and then lower heat so that it is barely simmering – if too fierce the gnocchi will break up. Add a teaspoonful of the mixture at a time to the stock. Allow to simmer for 3–4 minutes – *never longer as they will get too hard.*

These increase considerably in size as the semolina cooks in the stock, so do not overdo the size.

Serve with a sprinkling of grated cheese.

Gnocchi Verde o 'Strangola Preti'
Green Dumplings or 'Priest-stranglers'

These are so called because it seems a certain Don Giacometo who loved this delicacy choked and died while in the middle of eating it.

1lb 2oz/500g fresh or frozen spinach, cooked,
drained, squeezed dry and minced.
4oz/100g butter
6oz/180g ricotta cheese
7oz/200g stale bread, soaked in about
18fl oz/½ litre milk and strained
2 eggs
mixed flour and dried breadcrumbs (if necessary)
seasoning to taste
Parmesan cheese, grated

Sauté the spinach in half the butter till it seems as if it is about to stick to the pan. Add the ricotta and cook for 3 minutes.

Remove this mixture from the pan and place in a large bowl. Add the strained bread mixture and eggs and mix well. The mixture should now be firm but not dry. Add a little flour and breadcrumb mix if too moist. Season to taste.

Drop teaspoonsful in simmering (just off the boil) salted water. When the balls rise to the surface drain, toss them in butter and sprinkle with Parmesan cheese.

4 CARNE

Beef, Pork, Lamb and Mutton, Veal, Poultry and Game, Other

Venice and the Veneto, up until fifty years or so ago, did not eat as much beef and veal as they do today. Pork was more popular because it was produced in the area. The mainstay was, however, game and birds of every type, with various sauces to go with them and cooked with different herbs and spices. Cold cuts as well, of every type, were and still are very popular.

Beef

Pastizzada de Manzo
'Stewed' (Braised) Meat

This could be called a stew, but it's a more elaborately prepared dish and the meat is not cut into pieces but left whole.

Fresh polenta can be made the next day and the leftover meat eaten cold with the hot polenta, which makes a very palatable contrast.

Antonio Canova, famous sculptor of the eighteenth century, who was born in Possagno 50 miles from Venice, created his acclaimed 'Venere Vincitrice' with Poalina, wife of Prince Camillo Borghese as model. The prince arranged a sumptuous banquet in honour of Canova. There were whole peacocks presented with their beautiful feathers, huge lobsters on an imitation seabed of vegetables, whole pigs stuffed with birds and rare wines. Canova was obviously embarrassed so the prince enquired if he was not happy with the fare. Canova replied that he was a simple man who had retained his simple tastes and would like some polenta with *sugo di carne in*

umido – gravy from stewed meat. Poalina asked if she might taste some of this dish and declared that the yellow stuff with gravy was exquisitely incredible!

2lb 3oz/1kg lean beef
3oz/80g lard or fat or bacon
35fl oz/1 litre dry red wine
1 onion, chopped
1 carrot
1 stalk celery
2 cloves garlic
a few cloves
a sprig fresh rosemary
some stick-cinnamon
salt and black pepper

Make various incisions all over the meat and into these put the garlic, cloves, cinnamon and bacon, if using bacon. Place it in an earthenware dish or fireproof glass dish. Pour all the wine over the meat and add the rest of the ingredients.

Leave to marinade for at least a day, turning frequently. Remove from the marinade and, if bacon has not been used, lard or fat it all over. Replace in marinade and slowly bring to boil, lower heat and simmer slowly for 2–3 hours, covered, on stove.

Near the end of the 2–3 hours (whenever the meat is tender), mash or sieve or mouli the vegetables to give the gravy a thicker consistency.

This is served with yellow or white polenta.

Manzo in Umido
Beef in a Stewed Sauce

1½lb/700g beef or a mixture of beef, pork and/or veal
2 carrots, finely diced
1 stalk celery, finely diced

1 large onion, finely diced
2 cloves garlic, bruised
1 sprig fresh rosemary
1 pinch nutmeg
½ cup white wine
stock (about 1 cup)
seasoning
2oz/50g butter

Sauté all the ingredients together except the meat, till tender. Add the meat and brown. Add the wine and stock. Cover and simmer slowly till tender, adding more stock if liquid decreases too much.

The sauce of this is often served with pasta as a first course, and then the meat and sauce are served with boiled potatoes as a main course.

Manzo Brasato
Braised Beef

1lb 2oz–1lb 8oz/500–700g piece of beef
2oz/50g butter
1 glass white wine
3 tblspns tomato, peeled and sieved or mashed
salt and black pepper
1 clove garlic, bruised (optional)

Ask the butcher to tenderize the meat with a wooden meat tenderizer or do it at home. Season the meat very lightly and place in a pan with the already melted butter and cover the pan with a tight-fitting lid.

Braise the meat very gently till golden in colour. Sprinkle with the flour and add the wine and the tomato a little at a time, while continuing to braise the meat, until it is tender.

Serve with polenta.

50

Milkseller - from the Great Arch of San Marco

Manzo Rodolà
Rolled Beef

2lb 3oz/1kg lean beef, flattened
into a rectangular shape
1 carrot
1 onion
1 stalk celery
2 cloves garlic
2 leaves fresh sage
18fl oz/½ litre (approx) milk
½ cup grappa or brandy
seasoning

Finely chop together the carrot, celery, onion and sage till almost a paste and season. Spread this all over one side of meat and roll the meat up lengthwise, with the paste on the inside, tying with string at various intervals, and season.

Brown in the butter with the garlic.

Cover with the milk and cook in the oven at about 350°F/180°C. Halfway through the cooking time (after about ¾ hour) add the grappa or brandy then cook till tender and the milk has almost been consumed.

Polpette
Meatballs

11oz/300g (approx) any leftover meat
2oz/50g salami or sopressa
2oz/50g cooked ham
½ onion, finely chopped
breadcrumbs, fresh, to bind
breadcrumbs, dried
1 egg
a pinch of nutmeg
seasoning
oil for frying
a sprig of rosemary
1 clove garlic, bruised

Mince or very finely chop the meat, salami and ham together. Mix in the breadcrumbs, onion, egg and seasonings. Adjust amount of breadcrumbs if too soft. Roll mixture into balls and flatten slightly. Roll in dried breadcrumbs.

Fry in oil which has a sprig of rosemary and a bruised clove of garlic added. Drain well.

Rosbif in Cassariola
Roast Beef Casserole

3lb 5oz/1½kg boned sirloin (or topside if pot-roasting)
2oz/50g fatty bacon
1 finger-length stalk rosemary
seasoning
garlic cloves, quartered
2oz/50g (approx) butter

Stick small pieces of the garlic, bacon and rosemary in the beef at intervals. Place the beef in a casserole dish, lightly season and spread the butter over the meat. Cover with greaseproof or brown paper and place in oven at 325°F/160°C or on top of stove-burner at medium heat. Turn and baste from time to time.

Cooking time for medium rare is about 1 hour and 40 minutes. After this time the roast should be nicely browned on the outside and pink in the centre.

Serve with puréed potatoes (see Vegetables).

Goulasch
Goulash

This recipe is an inheritance from the nineteenth-century Austrian invasion.

1lb 2oz/½kg stewing beef, cubed
1 pinch aniseed
1 pinch marjoram
3 cloves garlic, peeled
2 pieces of lemon rind
3 carrots, grated coarsely
5–7oz/150–200g onions, finely diced
3 tblspns oil
½ tspn sweet paprika
½ tspn (or to taste) hot/piquant paprika
2 tblspns tomato sauce (see Sauces) or bought sauce

Finely chop together the aniseed, marjoram, garlic and lemon (or place in a blender). Mix with grated carrots. Heat the oil in a casserole dish and gently sauté onions till tender and golden. Add the finely chopped herbs and carrots and meat and brown meat well turning mixture often.

Simmer this all slowly till the sauce is a nice colour. Add the paprikas and the tomato sauce and simmer till the meat is tender – about 2½ hours.

Remove the meat and sieve the vegetables or blend the sauce till creamy. Add the meat and serve.

Bistecche Impanae
Crumbed steaks

Veal and pork steaks and flattened chicken breasts can be done in exactly the same way. The steaks of any type of meat must be thoroughly dried with absorbent paper beforehand to ensure that the egg and breadcrumbs adhere to their surface and do not break away when frying.

4 thinly sliced steaks (rump or any other cut)
½ cup Parmesan or other 'hard' cheese
½ cup dried breadcrumbs
oil for frying
1 clove garlic, bruised
seasoning
1 beaten egg
4 lemon wedges

Beat the egg and add seasoning. Mix the cheese and breadcrumbs together. Dip the steaks into the egg and then coat with the breadcrumb mixture. Heat oil with garlic and fry steaks till coating is golden-brown. Drain on absorbent paper.

Serve with lemon wedges.

Pork

Porseo al Latte
Pork in Milk

2lb 3oz/1kg lean pork
2oz/50g butter
35fl oz/1 litre (plus) milk
18fl oz/½ litre dry white wine
some sage leaves
1 sprig fresh rosemary
seasoning

Marinade the pork in the white wine for a couple of days turning every now and then.

Ponte di San Felice

Remove from wine and brown in the butter till golden in colour. Add the rest of the ingredients to pan and cover the pork completely with the milk. Simmer on top of the stove or in the oven. This must cook very slowly at a low temperature.

Near the end of the cooking period, when the pork is almost done, increase the heat in order to reduce the liquid.

This dish is served sliced, with its sauce over the sliced pieces.

___

Cotolete de Bosegato al Vin
Pork Chops with Wine Sauce

Bosegato is the Chioggia dialect name for pork – *porseo* in Venetian dialect. As can be seen dialects differ from island to island! Naturally this is a recipe from Chioggia.

4 pork chops
1 tblspn butter
1 tblspn flour
1 glass white wine
seasoning
1 heaped tblspn chopped parsley

Fry the chops in the butter. When done, remove and put aside to keep warm.

Mix the flour, wine and seasoning with the butter in which the pork was fried. Heat gently stirring constantly. Sprinkle the parsley over the chops and then pour sauce over them. Serve hot.

___

Bosegato Rostio su'l Speo
Spit-roast Suckling Pig

1 suckling pig, ready for roasting
3½oz/100g butter mixed with a handful of
chopped parsley
2 whole onions, with one clove stuck into each
seasoning
the pig's liver, finely chopped
a little lard
salted water and long rosemary branch for basting

for sauce:
1 tblspn chopped parsley
1 clove garlic
1 white onion
1 egg yolk
fresh cooking oil

Place all main ingredients in the cleaned stomach of the pig and secure opening with skewers or by sewing with strong thread. Tie the pig so its legs are close to the body. Place securely on the spit. Turn slowly. Using a long piece of rosemary branch as a basting brush, brush the pig with salted water till it starts turning golden. Continue basting with some lard speared on a fork. Remove when thoroughly cooked through.

Prepare sauce for serving. In a liquidizer (or pestle and mortar) place garlic clove, parsley and onion and blend till almost creamy white. Add egg yolk and, slowly beating, add a thin stream of oil, as one would to make mayonnaise. Continue till it is a good gravy consistency. Serve with the pork.

___

Carpaccio

This dish was named after the Venetian artist who lived from 1450 to 1523. It was invented at the time of Carpaccio's much-talked-about exhibition in Venice, by Giuseppe Cipriani, owner of Harry's Bar in Venice, for the Countess Amalia Nani Mocenigo who had been put on a severe diet by doctors. The reddish colour of the sauce recalls the reds of the artist's paintings.

per person:
4oz/100g thinly sliced fillet
steak (raw) as thin as Parma ham, so that it is
transparent (veal may be also used)

sauce (per person):
2 tblspns mayonnaise
1 tspn tomato purée
1 tspn Worcestershire sauce
¼ tspn dry mustard
1 tspn of whisky or brandy
3 tspns cream or yoghurt
3 drops tabasco sauce
a little pepper to taste

Mix all the sauce ingredients together. Chill till needed.

Arrange thinly sliced raw steak on a plate and serve sauce in a lettuce leaf.

___

Carpaccio con Salsa Maffioli
Carpaccio with Maffioli Sauce

Maffioli sauce is a variation of the above, invented by the late Giuseppe Maffioli, a well known gastronomic authority.

Instead of using tomato for this sauce, use instead offcuts of smoked salmon (ask your local delicatessen). Blend about ¾–1oz/20–30g (enough to give a delicate pink colour) together with the cream. Omit the mustard and tabasco.

___

Costesine de Maial
Pork Spare Ribs

14–20 spare ribs cut into finger-length pieces
4 sprigs rosemary, with stalks removed
2 tblspns sage leaves
1 tblspn ginger
4 cloves garlic, finely chopped

Musicians from "Saint George Baptizes the Heathens" (after Vittore Carpaccio)

Place the spare ribs on a grid over a large pan (in order that the excess fat may drip into the pan and that ribs do not cook in this fat). Season them with salt, pepper, garlic and ginger. Place the sage and rosemary leaves on top of the ribs.

Heat oven to 400–425°F/200–250°C and place ribs in oven. Turn frequently till ribs are crisp and done.

Serve with creamed potatoes.

Osei Scampai
Meat Skewers ('Flown Birds')

1lb 2oz/½kg of equal amounts
of cubed (¾in/1½cm) veal and pork
(for 8 skewers with 4 pieces on each)
32 sage leaves
40 small pieces of bacon (green), cut on the thick side
seasoning
2oz/50g butter
2 tblspns chopped parsley
½ cup dry white wine

To make skewers, slide on a piece of bacon, sage leaf, veal, sage leaf, bacon, pork. Repeat, ending with bacon.

Heat butter in a large pan and sauté the filled skewers till nicely browned. Add the wine and seasoning to taste and gently simmer, covered, till tender. Add a little water if necessary.

Serve with the gravy juices.

Lamb and Mutton

Agneleto Frito
Fried Lamb

This is delicious!

1lb 5oz/600g lamb, any cut, cut into pieces and pounded well
or 8 medium or 12 small chops
2 eggs
2 tblspns Parmesan cheese, grated,
or any other hard cheese
breadcrumbs
a good pinch of cinnamon
seasoning
oil for cooking

Mix the breadcrumbs, seasoning to taste, cheese and cinnamon together. Beat the eggs well.

Heat the oil and then dip the lamb pieces first into the egg then into the breadcrumb mix, coating them well.

Fry in hot oil till golden-brown and cooked through. Drain and dry on absorbent paper before serving.

Agneleto Rosto
Roast Lamb

1 leg of lamb or shoulder joint (ask your butcher for appropriate size for the amount of people)
seasoning
cooking oil
1 rosemary sprig
2 cloves garlic, finely chopped
4 sage leaves
2 glasses white wine

Salt and pepper the joint by rubbing all over with the seasonings. Lightly coat the joint with cooking oil. Place the garlic, sage and rosemary on top of joint. Place the joint in a moderate oven (or pot-roast on top of stove). Baste the joint often and add the wine halfway through roasting time.

When the joint is tender and done to a turn, remove and keep warm and deglaze pan juices by adding more liquid, to make a gravy.

Castra in Umido
Stewed Mutton

1lb 2oz/½kg mutton
1 tblspn butter
1 rasher of bacon or small piece leaf lard (squares of lard), diced
1 stalk celery, chopped
1 carrot, chopped
3 dried figs, plumped out in hot water and then finely chopped
½ glass white wine
1 glass water or stock
seasoning to taste

Sauté the mutton in the butter or lard, browning well. Add the rest of the ingredients except the wine. Cover the pot with a well fitting lid and slowly simmer till tender. Add a little water or stock from time to time if necessary. When just done, add the wine and leave to cook for another five minutes. Adjust seasoning.

Castradina
Salted, Smoked, Dried Mutton

This is an ancient, traditional recipe, still in use. It is eaten on the day of the Madonna della Salute (Madonna of Health), 21 November.

1lb 2oz/½kg salted, smoked mutton
(ask your butcher to do this if you do not have a smoker)
3 carrots, cleaned
1 onion, whole
1 potato
1 stalk celery
water to cover
seasoning

Cut the meat into pieces. Boil together with all the ingredients for at least 1½ hours and allow to cool for 10–12 hours. Remove the fatty layer from the stock and discard.

The stock is adjusted for seasoning and then served with tiny soup pasta and a sprinkling of cheese.

The mutton is served hot or cold with puréed potatoes and boiled carrots.

Rio di San Severo

Sally Spector 1985

Calle del Luganegher

Capretto con Agio Arosto
Kid Roasted with Garlic

This is a recipe from the 1300s.

1 oven-ready kid (if too much for your family, use half)
lard strips
5 cloves of garlic
juice of 1 lemon
2–3 egg yolks
2 cloves garlic
a little pepper
5fl oz/150ml stock

Lard the kid by inserting strips into the flesh at intervals and also insert the garlic at intervals. Place the kid on a spit-roast in your oven or on a grid, with a catchpan underneath. Blend all the rest of the ingredients and place in catchpan.

Roast at 400°F/200°C for same time as for chicken or lamb or until juices run clear, brushing the meat very often with the mixture in the catchpan. Serve with remaining juice.

Castrato Arosto
Mutton or Lamb Roast

This is a recipe from the 1500s.

1 leg of lamb or mutton
5 cloves
5 small pieces of cinnamon
5 sage leaves
2 sprigs rosemary
3½fl oz/100ml wine must (10½ oz/300ml wine and 1 tblspn honey, boiled till reduced by a third)
3½fl oz/100ml vinegar
4fl oz/125ml lamb stock
seasoning
a pinch of cinnamon and powdered cloves
a few slices of candied lemon and orange finely chopped

Insert the cloves, cinnamon, sage and rosemary leaves at random into the flesh of the lamb. Place meat on a spit or grid with catchpan underneath. Mix all the remaining ingredients together and place in catchpan in a moderate oven. Brush the leg often till juices run free and leg is done.

Serve with the sauce in the catchpan.

Veal

Vedel Stufa
Stewed Veal

1lb 2oz/½kg veal pieces for stewing, floured
seasoning
2oz/50g butter
1 glass white wine
1 glass water
1 sprig rosemary
1 clove garlic
2 onions, diced
2 carrots, diced
2 potatoes, diced
a pinch nutmeg
1 tblspn lemon juice

Sauté the floured veal in the butter till nicely browned. Add rest of the ingredients except the vegetables. Simmer for about 2 hours. Add the vegetables and simmer till they are tender.

Vedel in Umido
Veal in Herb Sauce

1lb 2oz/½kg veal cut into medium-sized pieces
for braising
2oz/50g butter
1 tblspn flour
1 onion, diced
1 clove garlic, bruised
½ teacup tomato purée (*not* concentrate)
1 glass white wine
1 tblspn parsley, finely chopped
3 sage leaves
3 basil leaves
a little cooking oil

Brown meat in the butter. Add the oil, onion and flour and sauté till onion is transparent and tender. Add the garlic and leave to cook for a few minutes. Add the tomato purée and wine. When the wine has been consumed, add the water and the basil and sage. Simmer, covered, till the meat is tender. A few minutes before removing from the heat, add the parsley.

CALLE DEL
LUGANEGHER

1129

Sally Spector 1987

Cotolete de Vedel Frite
Fried Veal Chops

See recipe for Fried Lamb Chops at the beginning of the Lamb and Mutton section.

Rodoleti de Vedel al Late
Rolled Veal Slices cooked in Milk

8 small, thinly sliced, veal steaks
½ cup hard cheese or soft mozarella, sliced
8 slices of cooked ham
8 small slivers of anchovies (optional but very good)
18fl oz/½ litre (approx) milk
seasoning (if using anchovies take these into account)
1 tblspn butter

Sprinkle each steak with seasoning and add cheese, a piece of ham and an anchovy. Roll up and secure with a toothpick. Sauté in butter, then while cooking add milk a little at a time till meat is tender.

Rodoletti de Vedel col Pien
Stuffed Veal Rolls

8 thin slices of veal

2oz/50g salami or sopressa
3½oz/100g ham or leftover meat
3 slices of bread, soaked in milk
1 beaten egg
2 tblspns finely chopped parsley
1 good pinch nutmeg
1 good pinch cinnamon
½ cup hard cheese, grated

1 carrot, finely chopped
1 stalk celery, finely chopped
1 onion, finely chopped
1 sprig rosemary
1 clove garlic, bruised
1 cup wine
seasoning to taste

Chop and blend well together all the ingredients from the salami to the cheese. Divide into 8 parts and place one on each veal steak. Roll up the steaks and secure with toothpick. Sauté in the butter till golden and then add the rest of the ingredients. Cover and simmer slowly for about one hour or till tender.

Scalopine
Veal Steaks

4 thin veal steaks
juice of a lemon
1 onion, finely chopped
1 tblspn butter
2 tblspns finely chopped parsley
flour
seasoning

Have your butcher flatten the veal steaks. Dry with absorbent paper and dust with seasoned flour. Melt the butter in a large pan and sauté the onion till tender. Add the steaks, parsley and lemon juice and cook for 4 minutes. Serve immediately.

Scalopine al Late
Veal Steaks Cooked in Milk

4 veal steaks
1 cup milk
1 cup Edam-type cheese, grated
4 slices ham (optional)
2oz/50g butter
seasoning

Marinade the seasoned veal for 2 hours in the milk. Just before the veal is to be served, remove and coat with flour. Melt the butter in a large pan and sauté the steaks till browned.

Sprinkle each steak with a little cheese – if using ham too, then first place a piece of ham on the steaks and then the cheese.

Add the milk and simmer slowly, covered, till milk has been consumed and has thickened.

Campo della Beccheria – Rialto Market

CATO DEL PESCE
AL MINVTO

CAMPO DE LE
BECCARIE

Scalopine al Marsala
Veal Steaks in Marsala

4 large veal steaks
1 tblspn flour
2 tblspns butter
½ cup Marsala
2 tblspns stock or water
seasoning

Sprinkle the steaks with the seasoning and lightly dust with the flour. Melt the butter in a large pan. When nicely hot, place the steaks in the butter and brown on both sides over a high heat. Add the Marsala and cook 1 minute more over the heat. Place meat in a serving dish and keep warm. Add stock or water to deglaze pan juices and pour over steaks. Serve immediately.

Ossibuchi alla Veneta
Ossobuco Veneta

Ossobuco is veal shinbone or hollowbone.

4 large (¾in/1½cm) shinbone with marrow, floured
3 carrots, finely diced
2 stalks celery, finely diced
2 onions, finely chopped
2 tblspns chopped parsley
1 cup white or red wine
or ½ cup wine with ½ cup water or stock
3 tblspns butter
1 tblspn oil
1 tblspn lemon juice (optional)

Melt butter and oil in a heavy-bottomed large pot and add floured meat. Brown all over on both sides turning often and carefully so that the bone does not come away from the meat. (A strong thread may be tied around the meat and bone to prevent them from parting.) When nicely browned, add the wine and continue cooking. When the wine has been half consumed add the finely chopped vegetables and the stock and simmer for 1 hour, adding more stock or water if necessary.

Five minutes before serving, add the parsley and lemon juice.

The vegetables should have made a lovely tasty 'sauce' and the meat and gravy should not be dry.

Vedel uso Ton
Veal used as Tuna

1lb 2oz/½kg lean veal roast
2 tblspns oil
2 tblspns butter
1 clove garlic
1 bayleaf
3½oz/100g beef marrow
salt
juice of a ½ lemon
2 salted sardines
or 4 anchovies without bones, well chopped
1 cup water

Place oil, butter, garlic, bayleaf, beef marrow and a little salt over the veal roast and place in a roasting pan. Place in the preheated oven set at 400°F/200°C and roast slowly, basting with a little hot water from time to time till the veal is tender.

Meanwhile mix together the remaining ingredients. Then pour this over the veal roast in the last 15 minutes of its cooking time. Leave for 7 minutes then turn the roast over and baste with the sardine or anchovy water. Leave for 8 minutes then remove the roast and keep warm. Use juices to make a gravy, adding pepper to taste and a little flour if desired.

Serve sliced, with sauce poured over.

Vedel Toná
Tunnied Veal

This is a very good buffet dish. Chicken or turkey slices can also be used.

1lb 2oz/½kg veal roast (lean), roasted as above or your normal way

for sauce:
3½oz/100g (approx) tin tuna fish
6 anchovies
1 tspn lemon juice
6 capers
9fl oz/250ml mayonnaise
2fl oz/50ml cream
pepper to taste

gherkins
capers

Thinly slice the veal and arrange on a large serving dish. In a blender or liquidizer blend all the sauce ingredients together forming a not too thick sauce. Pour over veal.

Decorate with more capers and some gherkin fans.

RIO DE LE
ERBE

Poultry and Game

Polastro Impaná
Crumbed chicken

1 chicken, cut into 8 pieces and flattened
seasoning
flour
1–2 eggs, beaten with a little milk and salt to taste
1 pinch cinnamon (optional)
breadcrumbs
oil for frying
1 tblspn chopped parsley

Dry the chicken pieces and coat with seasoned flour. Dip into egg mixture and then coat with breadcrumbs. (If using the cinnamon, add this to the breadcrumbs.) Fry in hot oil over medium heat till both sides are golden-brown. Sprinkle with the parsley and serve with a salad.

Petti de Polo Impaná
Crumbed Chicken Breasts

4 chicken-breast steaks
flour
1–2 eggs, beaten
1 cup breadcrumbs, *mixed with*
½ cup hard cheese, grated, *and*
1 good pinch nutmeg
seasoning
oil
4 lemon wedges

Ask your butcher to flatten the steaks. (Each chicken-breast half is sliced into two and flattened between two pieces of waxed paper.) Coat steaks with flour and season. Dip into the egg and then into the breadcrumb mixture, coating well. Then fry in hot oil over a medium heat till nicely golden. Garnish with lemon wedges.

Polastro in Tecia
Pan-cooked Chicken

1 chicken, cut into 8 pieces
1 tblspn oil
1 tblspn butter
seasoning
1 onion, chopped
½ garlic clove, chopped
1 tblspn chopped parsley
3 sage leaves
1 chicken's liver and heart
1 tblspn tomato concentrate diluted in
½ cup boiling water
2 glasses dry white wine

Sauté the chicken pieces in the oil and butter till golden in colour. Meanwhile blend or pound the onion, garlic, parsley, sage, seasoning and chicken liver and heart together. Put this mixture on top of the browned chicken pieces and add the diluted tomato concentrate.

Simmer the chicken slowly adding the wine a little at a time. If the sauce is too liquid add a little flour to thicken slightly.

Polastro a la Buranea
Burano Chicken

This is an excellent dish.

1 chicken cut into 4 or 8 pieces *or* 8 thighs
1 tspn vinegar
2 carrots, finely chopped
1 stalk celery, finely chopped
1 large onion, finely chopped
1 clove garlic, finely chopped
4 green olives, finely chopped
5 capers, finely chopped
3 sage leaves, chopped
1 tblspn rosemary, chopped
1 sausage, finely chopped
2 rashers bacon, finely chopped
2 tblspns oil
½ cup white wine
juice of ½ lemon
1 piece lemon peel
1 tot brandy

Place the chicken in a large bowl of water with the vinegar. Leave to stand for ½ hour.

Meanwhile mix together the chopped carrots, celery, onion, garlic, olives, capers, sage, rosemary, sausage and bacon.

In a large pan heat the oil and place the chicken pieces, dried, and the vegetables together in the hot oil. Reduce heat to the minimum and slowly simmer till it all becomes golden in colour, turning every now and then. Add the wine, lemon juice, lemon peel and brandy. Mix well. Put a lid on the pan and simmer till chicken is tender.

Serve with polenta or boiled rice.

Crest of Murano – cock and serpent

Polastro in Gelatina
Chicken in Aspic

1 boiled chicken
3½oz/100g sliced tongue
5oz/150g cooked ham
1 small bottle of mushrooms in oil
½ stalk celery, very finely chopped
seasoning
6 walnuts, finely chopped
1 pkt gelatine *or* 3 sheets isinglass
18fl oz/½ litre chicken stock

to decorate:
artichoke hearts in oil (*see* recipe in Antipasti section)
stuffed olives
parsley sprigs

to serve:
mayonnaise

Remove all the meat from the bones and dice together with the ham and tongue, and mix with the mushrooms, celery and walnuts. Season.

Make up the gelatine and pour some of this into an oiled 2 pint/1 litre mould to make a thinnish layer. Put into freezer or fridge for a quick set.

Then pack meat mixture on top taking special care not to let it get too close to the sides of the mould. Pour the rest of the gelatine down the sides of the mould and all over the meat and leave to set. This should take about 5 hours.

When ready to serve, unmould chicken by dipping mould into a bowl of hot water quickly and turning out on to slightly wet plate. (This makes it easier to move if not quite in centre.)

Decorate with the artichokes which have been slightly opened in the middle to resemble a flower with a whole or half an olive in the centre with stuffing side up. Garnish with sprigs of parsley and serve with a gravy boat of mayonnaise at hand.

Polastri Pini e Boni
Chicken Stuffed with Almonds, Herbs and Cheese

This was most successful when I prepared it at the Cipriani Hotel in Venice. The recipe dates from the 1300s.

1 chicken (approx 3½lb/1½kg), cleaned
3½oz/100g almonds, blanched and ground
2 eggs
9oz/250g caciotta or soft cheese
1 tblspn mixed finely minced parsley, rosemary, marjoram, basil and sage
a pinch each of pepper, cinnamon, ginger, nutmeg and saffron
a little almond milk or normal milk to bind if needed
salt and pepper to taste

Mix or blend all the ingredients except the chicken, adding a little milk to obtain a soft consistency.

Separate the skin from the chicken by pushing your hands between the breasts and skin and working round to the back and into the legs too. Take care not to break the skin.

Spread the stuffing between the flesh and skin and fill the cavity well, remembering the stuffing will expand with cooking. Stitch up the cavity with kitchen twine. Brush chicken with oil and roast at 375°F/190°C allowing 20 minutes per 1lb/½kg plus an extra 20 minutes, or until juices run clear when thigh is pierced. Allow to stand for 10 minutes before serving.

We used to serve this deboned completely for easier carving.

Pollastri Arosti
Roast Chicken

This is a recipe from the 1300s.

1 oven-ready chicken
1 tblspn oil
seasoning
1 sprig rosemary
juice of 1 pomegranate or orange or lemon
3 tblspns rosewater
1 tspn sugar
a pinch of cinnamon

Roast the chicken at 375°F/190°C with the oil, rosemary and seasoning allowing 20 minutes for each 1lb/½kg and 20 minutes over. Fifteen minutes minimum before done add the rest of the ingredients.

Ale alla Chiozota
Turkey Wings Chioggia

This recipe dates from 1819. It can be made with chicken wings, but you will need more of them.

4–8 turkey wings, depending on your family's or
friends' appetites
2oz/50g melted butter
1 tblspn flour
3½fl oz/100ml vinegar
3½fl oz/100ml water or stock
salt to taste
a little basil
½ clove garlic
1 slice of onion
1 finger length of carrot
3 cloves
3 bayleaves
1 tblspn parsley
a little zest of orange
1–2 egg whites, beaten
flour
oil for frying
parsley for garnish

Heat a little till tepid the butter, flour, vinegar, stock, salt, garlic, cloves, onion, carrot, bayleaves, parsley, zest, basil. Place in a large bowl and marinade the wings in this for four hours, turning regularly.

Remove wings and dry on asborbent towels. Dip them into the beaten egg whites and then into the flour and fry in hot oil. Serve with more parsley.

Polastra Rosta
Roast Chicken

1 chicken (3lb 5oz/1½kg)
rosemary
sage
garlic, bruised or crushed
salt
1 tblspn oil
1 generous teaspoon grated lemon peel

Place pieces of sage, rosemary and garlic in cavity of chicken. Rub salt all over chicken. Sprinkle oil over and roast as normal till golden and tender. Make gravy by deglazing pan juices with a little water, stock, brandy or wine and add the grated lemon peel to it.

Petti de Polo al Parsuto
Chicken Breasts with Ham

4 chicken breasts/steaks, flattened
4 slices cooked ham
1½ cups grated soft cheese
or 4 small mozzarella, sliced
1 tblspn oil
1 tblspn butter
juice 1 lemon
seasoning
white wine (optional)

Sauté the seasoned chicken pieces on one side in the oil and butter till golden. Remove from the heat, turn over, golden side up, and place a piece of ham, and a quarter of the cheese over the ham, on each piece.

When all have been prepared this way, sprinkle the lemon juice over them. Place lid on pan and simmer till tender.

A little white wine may be added with the lemon juice.

Anara in Tecia
Pan-cooked Duck

1 duck (3lb 5oz/1½kg), cut into 8 pieces
1 stalk celery, finely chopped
1 onion, finely chopped
1 green pepper, finely chopped
seasoning
1 cup white wine
1 cup stock
flour
½ tblspn butter

Melt the butter in a pan – nonstick if possible – and brown the duck pieces. This prebrowning also allows the duck's excess natural fats to be removed. Remove the pieces, drain some of the fat out of the pan, leaving 1 tblspn. Sauté the vegetables in this till tender and then add duck pieces.

Add the stock and wine a little at a time throughout the cooking period (1½–2 hours) till meat is tender. Thicken sauce if necessary with a little flour and check seasoning.

Anara Rosta
Roast Duck

The duck in this recipe is cooked in the same way as the 'Roast Chicken' recipe above.

Ponte dei Tre Archi

Anara col Pien
Stuffed Duck

1 duck (3lb 5oz/1½kg), cleaned
1 duck's liver and heart
2oz/50g sopressa (salami)
2oz/50g Parmesan cheese, grated
1 tblspn chopped parsley
1 egg, beaten
seasoning
1 tspn nutmeg
1 piece undercut of tuna (optional)
1 slice bread, dipped in milk
1 tblspn butter
2 rashers bacon, diced
1 tblspn oil

Mince or blend or finely chop together the liver, heart, salami, cheese and parsley. Add the tuna if using. Add the egg, seasoning and nutmeg and knead together. Add enough bread dipped in milk to make a firm but moist stuffing. Fill the duck – but not too full as the stuffing expands when cooked. Close with a skewer. Sprinkle with the bacon, butter and oil.

Roast in a moderate oven till done (1½–2 hours). Remove and drain excess fat off. Make a gravy by deglazing the pan juices.

Anare Selvadeghe
Wild Duck

This is made in the same way as 'Chicken Burano' above.

Resti de Anara Rosta in Salmi
Leftover Roast Duck Salmi

This can also be made with any other type of poultry or bird.

leftover duck
2oz/50g butter
1 tblspn flour
1 onion, chopped
½ cup stock
½ cup red wine
seasoning
2 small pieces of lemon peel
1 tblspn chopped parsley
thyme and bayleaf in gauze bag

Melt the butter in a pan and add the flour and stir till golden in colour. Add the onion and after a few minutes, when tender, add the stock, wine and seasoning. Add the pieces of leftover bird with the lemon, thyme, bayleaf and parsley and simmer slowly for an hour. Remove the thyme and bayleaf.

Serve with toast.

Faraona coi Bisi
Guinea-Fowl with Peas

1 guinea-fowl, cleaned
2 tblspns butter
3 rashers bacon, chopped
1 cup chicken stock
1lb 2oz/½kg fresh or frozen peas
seasoning
1 sprig rosemary
2 sage leaves
2 cloves garlic, bruised

Sauté the bacon in the butter. Add the seasoned guinea-fowl. Over the heat add the stock a little at a time, keeping the fowl moist. When half cooked, add the peas, herbs and garlic and continue cooking in the oven at 325°F/160°C for 1½–2 hours till the guinea-fowl is well cooked and the peas tender.

Faraona co la Pevarada
Guinea-Fowl in a Piquant Sauce

1 guinea-fowl, cut into pieces or whole
1 tblspn oil
2 tblspns butter
3 rashers bacon, chopped
3 sage leaves
1 sprig rosemary
½ cup white wine
seasoning

sauce:
3 slices sopressa or salami
2–3 anchovy fillets
juice of 1 lemon and 1 tspn of its rind
juice of ½ orange and 1 tspn of its rind
1 tblspn chopped parsley
1 tblspn butter
1 tspn vinegar
4–5oz/100–150g chicken and guinea-fowl livers, finely chopped

Cover the breast of the guinea-fowl with the bacon, sage leaves and rosemary, and tie securely. Season. Sauté the fowl in the butter and oil, until nicely browned, then add the wine and simmer, uncovered, till tender.

Alternatively, roast whole in oven with all the rest of the main ingredients at 375°F/190°C for 20 minutes per 1lb/½kg plus 20 minutes, or until the juices run clear. Remove and cut into four and keep warm. Keep pan juices for sauce.

To make the sauce, sauté the sopressa, livers, parsley and anchovies in the butter, then add the orange juice and rind and lemon juice and rind. Add the vinegar and pan juices and cook through. Place in blender till almost smooth.

Osei e Polenta
Birds and Polenta

There's a saying in Venice '*polenta e osei, magnarli coi dei*', that means 'polenta and birds, food for the gods'.

4 small birds (quails, snipe, spatchcock or any other type of small bird)
4 tblspns butter
3 sage leaves
3 rashers bacon, diced
seasoning
made polenta (*see* Chapter 3)

Melt 2 tblspns butter in a pan and add the sage and bacon and sauté for a minute or two. On top of this put the birds. Season. Over a high heat cook the birds till done, about 20 minutes, taking care that they do not burn. Add the rest of the butter.

Prepare a serving dish with a layer of polenta and the birds and sauce placed on top of this. If the sauce seems too little, add a little more butter.

Colombi coi Bisi
Pigeons with Peas

This is sometimes also called 'foreign' pigeons with peas (*colombi foresti coi bisi*) because the pigeons used were not actually Venetian.

Sally Spector 1987

Venetians call anything which does not come, or is not grown, from its islands in the lagoon, 'foresto' (foreign) including people! During the war years, pigeons couldn't be found in Venice, because crafty housewives lured them from their balconies into their kitchen pots. During this period nobody restricted themselves to the old Venetian saying 'Mese de Agosto, colombo rosto' (month of August, pigeon roast).

4 small pigeons
4 small pieces of leaf lard or fat bacon
5oz/150g bacon, chopped
1 tblspn butter
½kg fresh or frozen peas
2 tblspns flour
2 glasses white wine
seasoning
2 tblspns (approx) parsley
1 bayleaf

Tie a piece of lard to each bird. Melt butter in a pan at medium heat and sauté birds till golden-brown. Remove pigeons and keep warm.

Add the bacon to the pan juices and cook a little. Remove this too. Add the flour to the pan juices till it becomes dark gold in colour and then add the wine, seasoning, parsley and bayleaf. Stir again, add the bacon which was removed and kept warm and the peas. When the peas are half cooked add the pigeons and simmer slowly till all is well cooked (about 1½ hours).

Venetian Lagoon, with Burano and Torcello in the Distance

Qualia col Pien Rosto
Stuffed Roast Quails

This is a recipe which was handed down to my mother-in-law.

4 quails
2 tblspns butter
2 tblspns oil
5oz/150g salami or mortadella or sopressa
3½oz/100g chicken livers
2 tblspns grated Parmesan cheese
1 egg
1 sprig rosemary, stalk removed
1 clove garlic
1 pinch nutmeg
fresh breadcumbs
a little stock
seasoning

Finely chop or blend together the salami, livers, cheese, rosemary leaves, garlic and nutmeg. Season and add the beaten egg and a few breadcrumbs to bind. Fill the birds and sew or skewer closed.

Melt the butter and oil and slowly simmer birds, adding stock from time to time. These birds cook quickly, in about 20 minutes. Use juices to make a gravy.

Serve with creamed potatoes.

Conicio in Umido
Stewed Rabbit

1 rabbit, cut into pieces
1 onion, chopped
2 tblspns oil
1 tblspn butter
1 rabbit's liver, heart etc, finely chopped
1 tblspn parsley
1 cup white wine
seasoning
juice of ½ lemon (optional)

Melt oil and butter and sauté the onion till nicely golden-brown. Season and add the rabbit pieces, liver etc and parsley. When this too is nicely browned add the wine and lemon, if using. Simmer till well done, about 1½–2 hours.

Serve with polenta or creamed potatoes.

Conicio a la Caciatora
Hunter's Rabbit

1 rabbit, cut into pieces
1 carrot, finely chopped
2 stalks celery, finely chopped
1 onion, finely chopped
1 clove garlic, bruised
1 tblspn oil
1 tblspn butter
5 sage leaves, chopped
1 sprig rosemary, stalk removed and leaves chopped
½ stock cube
pepper
a good pinch of nutmeg
2 tblspns white wine
2 tblspns brandy

Heat the butter and oil and sauté the vegetables and herbs till tender, taking care not to burn or brown them. Add the stock cube dissolved in a little water, pepper and nutmeg. Mix well and add the rabbit. Simmer slowly, adding first the wine and when this is consumed, water a little at a time. After 1½ hours or 15 minutes before it is to be served and the meat and vegetables are nicely cooked and tender, add the brandy.

Some of this sauce may also be used for the first-course pasta or gnocchi with extra butter and oil added and grated cheese.

The rabbit is served with the sauce, creamed potatoes and a salad.

Lievaro in Salmi
Hare Salmi or Jugged Hare

1 hare, cut into pieces
1½ cups red wine
1 onion, chopped
1 stalk celery, chopped
1 carrot, chopped
1 tblspn parsley, chopped
1 bayleaf
1 stalk thyme
1 sprig rosemary
3 sage leaves
½ tspn pepper
1 tblspn oil
1 tblspn butter
1 hare's liver, heart and gizzard, finely chopped
1oz/25g salami or sopressa, chopped
1 whole nutmeg *and*
1 piece of cinnamon *and*
3 cloves in a gauze bag
½ cup water
1 tspn lemon juice and peel from 1 lemon

Marinade the hare in the red wine, onion, celery, carrot, parsley and rest of herbs and let stand for 2–12 hours. Remove hare from bowl and in a large pan melt the butter with the oil. Salt and flour the hare and brown in the oil and butter. When it is slightly brown, add the herbs and vegetables from the marinade and continue browning. When well browned, add the marinade wine and continue cooking slowly till the wine evaporates. Add some water, the salami, liver, heart and gizzard, lemon peel and gauze bag and cover pan. Remove bag after 15 minutes. Add a tspn lemon juice and pepper. Cook till hare is well done (about 1½–2 hours).

Lievaro in Tocio
Hare in Herb Sauce

1 hare, cleaned, prepared and cut into pieces
1 tblspn vinegar
2 carrots
1 onion
1 stalk celery
1 sprig rosemary
2 sage leaves
1 tspn thyme
½ tspn marjoram
1 clove garlic
4 basil leaves
1 tblspn parsley
1 mint leaf
1 tblspn oil
1 tblspn butter
1 hare's liver, heart and gizzard, finely chopped
1 handful chopped parsley
2 cups white wine and water
1 tblspn orange rind

Place the hare in a bowl with the carrots, onion and celery, and water to cover mixed with the vinegar and leave to marinade for 24 hours. Remove and dry the meat and vegetables. Finely chop or blend the carrots, onion, celery, rosemary, sage, thyme, marjoram, garlic, basil, tblspn parsley and mint.

Put the hare in a pan and brown in the butter and oil. Add the chopped vegetables and herbs, together with the liver, heart, and gizzard. Brown these too, adding the wine and water a little at a time till it is consumed. Repeat till the hare is tender. Add more than the given amount of wine and water if necessary to make a nice sauce.

When the hare is cooked add the orange rind and handful of parsley and cook for 1–2 minutes more.

Other

Figà a la Venessiana
Venetian Liver

8 slices of liver (preferably veal), sliced thinly and cut into strips
4 medium onions, chopped
2 tblspns oil (preferably olive)
2 tblspns butter
seasoning to taste
½ glass brandy, red wine or Marsala
1 tspn grated lemon peel
2 tblspns chopped parsley

Melt oil and butter and sauté onions till transparent and tender – do not burn or over brown. Then, over a high heat, add the liver pieces and cook for a little while, stirring constantly. Add lemon peel, parsley and brandy or wine after five minutes cooking period and allow liquid to evaporate.

Serve immediately.

Cotolete de Figà a la Venessiana
Venetian Liver Steaks

4 large veal liver steaks
2 tblspns parsley, chopped
seasoning
1–2 beaten eggs
flour
breadcrumbs
3 tblspns butter
4 lemon wedges

Season the liver and place on a plate. Sprinkle the parsley over the steaks and leave to stand for ½ hour.

Ten minutes before the meal is to be served, lightly dust the steaks with flour, dip into the egg and then coat with breadcrumbs. Fry the steaks in the butter till both sides are golden-brown.

Serve with lemon wedges and garnish with parsley.

Cotolete de Figà al Marsala
Liver Steaks with Marsala

4 large liver steaks (preferably veal)
seasoning
flour
1 glass Marsala or red wine
3 tblspns butter

Season the liver steaks and then lightly flour them. Place the steaks in the melted butter and fry till golden-brown. Add the Marsala and simmer slowly for 10 minutes. Serve with the sauce.

Fongadina Venessiana
Venetian Lamb's Liver, Heart and Lungs

These are usually sold attached to the trachea in Venice. Ask your butcher to prepare yours separately if possible.

heart, liver and lungs of 1 lamb
2 tspns flour
1 tblspn butter
½ tblspn oil
1 onion, sliced
3 sprigs rosemary
seasoning

If bought as described above, remove the heart, liver and lungs from the trachea and discard the latter. Boil the lungs in salted water for 10 minutes calculating from the time it starts to boil. Drain reserving water.

In a pan (preferably nonstick), without adding any oil or butter, put the flour and, stirring all the time, brown. Add the oil and butter and then the onion. Cook the onion till tender but not golden.

In the meantime, slice and dice the lungs, heart and liver. Add the lungs first with the rosemary and cook for 15 minutes. Then add the heart and liver and cook for another 15 minutes. If the sauce becomes too dry add a little water in which the lungs were boiled.

This is served with polenta.

Lengua Salmistrada a la Venessiana
Venetian Salted Tongue

This is a very old recipe used to keep certain cuts of meat longer. In those days this dish was left in the coolest part of the house to marinade, usually as near water level as possible, and well covered.

1 ox tongue
salt
a pinch of saltnitrate (saltpetre) per 2lb/1kg weight
1 tblspn juniper seeds
1 tblspn rosemary leaves
1 tblspn garlic cloves
1 tblspn sage leaves
peppercorns

optional:
3 carrots
2 celery stalks
2 onions

optional:
piquant sauce (*see* Sauces)

Without washing the tongue, rub it all over with salt and saltnitrate. Place in an earthenware bowl and sprinkle generously with the juniper seeds, rosemary leaves, garlic cloves, sage leaves and peppercorns. Leave at the bottom of the fridge for minimum 15 days, maximum a month, turning every 2 days.

When ready to be eaten, remove it from bowl and wash very well in cold water. Then bring to steady boil in a pot of cold water without salt topping up water when necessary.

When tender (about 3 hours), remove from pot and remove the thick outer skin and cut into thick serving slices.

Some families like to boil the listed vegetables to give added flavour and to eat with the meat.

It can be served with the piquant sauce.

Lengua in Salsa
Veal Tongue with Anchovy Sauce

1 veal tongue
5 bayleaves
5 sage leaves
1 handful parsley
flour for dusting
oil for frying
4 anchovy fillets, minced
1 tblspn capers, minced
1 glass dry white wine

Boil the tongue in salted water together with the bayleaves, sage and parsley till tender. Remove and skin the tongue and cut into slices – not too thin. Dust well in flour and fry in oil till golden. Remove and keep warm.

Scrape all the remains from the bottom of the pan and strain through a fine strainer. Replace this sauce over heat and add the anchovies, the capers and the wine and simmer till a nice sauce is obtained. Pour over the tongue slices.

Latesini Friti
Fried Sweetbreads

1lb 2oz/½kg sweetbreads
1–2 eggs, beaten
flour
breadcrumbs
seasoning to taste
pinch nutmeg
½ cup oil, for frying

Prepare the sweetbreads as in previous recipe and cut into bite-size pieces. Roll these in the flour. Season them and then dip in the eggs and roll in the breadcrumbs mixed with the nutmeg. Fry till golden-brown. Remove and drain.

Tip: if breadcrumbs and nutmeg are put into a fairly large plastic bag and all the pieces of sweetbread placed on top of the crumbs, by holding the neck of the bag tightly closed and shaking well the pieces will separate and at the same time be well coated with the crumbs. Add more breadcrumbs if not enough.

Rognonsini al Marsala
Kidneys with Marsala

4 veal kidneys
or 1lb 2oz/½kg beef kidney
2 tblspns butter
1 tblspn chopped parsley
2 cloves garlic, finely chopped
1 cup Marsala or Madeira
seasoning to taste

Slice the kidneys thinly, removing any fat. Coat in flour. Sauté the parsley and garlic in the butter. Add the kidneys, seasoning and Marsala. Cook over a medium heat, not high, for 15 minutes.

Rognonsini Trifolai
Truffled Veal Kidneys

4 veal kidneys
2 cloves garlic, finely chopped
seasoning
1 tblspn butter
1 tblspn chopped parsley
juice of 1 lemon
1 tblspn oil

Cut the kidneys thinly, removing any fat. Heat the oil in the pan and when hot, add the kidneys and seasoning. Increase the heat and cook briskly for 5 minutes. Add butter, parsley and lemon juice and cook for about two minutes. Serve immediately.

Church of the Salute and Dogana da Mar (marine customs house)

Rognonsini ala Graela
Grilled Veal Kidneys

2 veal kidneys
2 tblspns olive oil
seasoning
3 tblspns lemon juice (reserve peel)

Slice the kidneys in half and remove the fat. Place in a large dish. Season and sprinkle with oil and leave for 1 hour.

Place kidneys on a hot grill and cook for 5–6 minutes on each side.

Place on a serving dish and add lemon and finely chopped peel.

Tripe de Porseo
Pork Tripe

1lb 12oz/800g pork tripe, cleaned
35fl oz/1 litre (approx) beef stock
1 tblspn olive oil
2 tblspns butter
1 onion, finely chopped
1 sprig rosemary
3 sage leaves
3 cloves
1 small piece stick-cinnamon
seasoning to taste

If the tripe has not been precooked when bought, then boil for 1 hour in plain water to remove bitterness and excess fat. Rinse with fresh water. Then place in a pot with the stock and simmer for 4–5 hours. Remove and cut into strips. Sauté the rest of ingredients together till onion is tender but still pale in colour. Add the tripe and sauté till golden in colour.

Luganeghette e Polenta
Italian Sausages and Polenta

1lb 2oz/½kg small Italian sausages (luganeghette)
made polenta (*see* Chapter 3)

Place sausages in a pan and cover with water. Cook over medium heat till water has been consumed (about 1 hour). This will leave enough fat behind in which to brown the sausages nicely and give them a lovely crust.

Serve with polenta.

Luganeghette e Fasoi
Sausages and Beans

1lb 2oz/½kg small Italian sausages
2 tblspns olive oil
1½ tblspns tomato concentrate
seasoning
4 cups cooked kidney beans, kept warm
1 sprig rosemary

Cook the sausages as above and when golden, remove from pan and keep warm. Add oil to fat and add tomato concentrate and seasoning and cook for 10 minutes. Add the sausages and rosemary and cook for 30 minutes more.

Place beans on bottom of serving dish and place the sausages on top of the beans. Pour the sauce over both. Put in a moderate oven for 5–10 minutes if desired.

Church of the Redentore

5 PESSE

Fish plays a large part in the cuisine of Venice and of the Veneto: in particular shellfish, eel, sardines and trout (from mountain lakes and rivers). The most popular ways of cooking fish are to deep fry, charcoal or open roast. Alongside fresh fish, *baccalà* (salted and dried cod) is also traditional to the region and after long soaking can be cooked in many different ways. The Adriatic is an enormous breeding ground for *vongole* (clams) and steps have been taken to prevent the illegal raking of the seabed when fishing which ruins not only the clams but also the eggs of other species.

The Adriatic, the lagoon and *padane* valley, offer numerous variety of fish, crustaceans and molluscs, many species being cultivated in enclosed breeding grounds in the Venetian estuary, for example eel, sole, crabs, scallops, mussels, John Dory, bass and soft-shell crabs.

To the tourist who comes to Venice, the wonderful meals of fresh fish make it a gourmet's

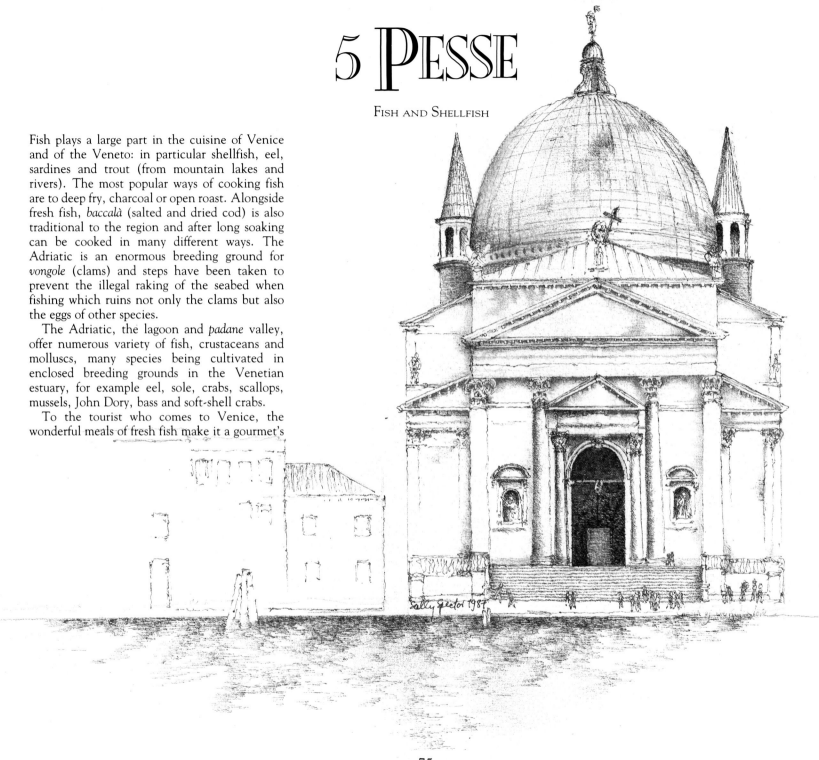

paradise. The visitor should explore further north of Venice as well, along the Po, as this is where the Po sturgeon is found. Its caviar is exquisite and much tenderer than that of the Russian type.

Under the Roman Empire much fish was eaten and they used sauces – much as we used stock cubes today – derived from the putrification of fish and their intestines, including a special one called *garum* and a lesser-quality one called *alec* or *murria*. With the decline of the Empire, fish continued to be popular in Venice and the town invented its own sauces, in particular one with anchovies or sardines, and one called *saor* (or *cisame de pesse* in the thirteenth century), which is still popular today.

Aziá coi Bisi
Dogfish with Peas

4 finger-thick fillets of dogfish, skinned
9oz/250g fresh or frozen peas
2 tblspns oil
1 onion, finely chopped
1 tblspn chopped parsley
1 tblspn tomato sauce (*see* Sauces)
or ½ tblspn tomato concentrate
seasoning

Heat the oil and sauté the onion and parsley till the onion is tender. Add the peas, tomato and enough water to cover. Simmer for 15 minutes, after which the peas should be tender.

Place the seasoned fillets in the pan with the peas and cook over a low heat for a few minutes. The sauce formed should be fairly thick.

This fish is very tender and does not need much cooking.

Aziá in Tecia
Pan-cooked Dogfish

8 thinly sliced fillets of dogfish, skinned and floured
3 tblspns oil
1 onion
1 tblspn parsley
2 cloves garlic
1 cup white wine
1 tblspn tomato sauce (*see* Sauces)
or tomato concentrate
seasoning

Finely chop or blend together the onion, parsley and garlic. Place in a pan with the oil and heat. When nicely hot, add the fillets, cooking first on one side and then the other. Then add the wine, tomato and seasoning and cook till wine is half consumed so that the sauce is not too liquid.

Aziá Frito
Fried Dogfish

4 fillets of dogfish, minium 3½oz/100g each, cleaned, skinned and dried
juice of 1 lemon
seasoning
flour
1–2 eggs, beaten
oil for frying
4 lemon wedges

Place the fillets in a dish, season and pour lemon juice over them and leave to stand for 20–30 minutes. Then flour them very well, dip them into the egg and fry in the hot oil. Serve garnished with lemon.

Anguele in Saor
Pickled or Soused Small Fish

2lb 3oz/1kg of any small fish such as anchovy, whitebait, sardine, herring or pilchard
flour
oil for frying
½ tspn peppercorns
vinegar (enough to cover fish)

Clean and then season and flour the fish. Heat the oil and fry them for a minute or two on each side till cooked through. Take care not to overcook. Drain well and place in a glass dish and cover with vinegar. Leave to marinade for at least 5 hours before eating. These are eaten cold.

Ragosta Lessa
Boiled Lobster

I don't believe in putting these creatures alive in boiling *court bouillon* as many do. It's much kinder to drown them in fresh water first or to pierce their heads with a sharp instrument near the eyes where the brain is situated.

2 medium lobsters
1 onion
1 stalk celery
1 carrot
1 tspn salt
2 tblspns vinegar

Place all the ingredients in a large pot of water – enough to cover the lobsters – except the lobsters, and bring to the boil. Put the (dead) lobsters in the boiling water and cook for 20 minutes. Cool in the water.

Take lobsters out and split open. Remove the stomach (near the head) and the long intestine attached to it. Remove the greenish-brown liver and discard the small antennae underneath the stomach. Crack the large claws with a knife or

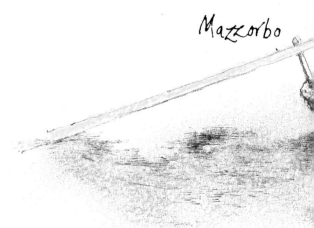

Mazzorbo

hammer and remove the flesh. Cut the lobster flesh into medallions (ie, cut the body meat into rounds like one does a carrot).

Serve in the shell with any suitable sauce, such as a seafood sauce, *béarnaise* sauce or tartar sauce.

Ragosta a la Diavola
Devilled Lobster

2 medium lobsters precooked as described above
2 tblspns oil
3 tblspns melted butter
½ cup vinegar
½ tspn pepper
5 (approx) red pepper (chilli) *seeds*, or more if desired
1 tspn beef stock
1 cup boiling water
1 tspn tomato concentrate
1 tspn flour
½ tspn prepared mustard

Cut the lobsters into two lengthwise. Place the lobsters, meat side up, in a baking tray. Sprinkle with 2 tblspns melted butter and oil and bake in hot oven for 10 minutes.

While the lobsters are baking make up the

sauce as follows. Place the vinegar, pepper and chilli seeds in a pot and simmer till vinegar has been reduced to half. Add the beef stock to the boiling water and add this together with the tomato concentrate to the vinegar and cook for 10 minutes. Mix 1 tblspn of melted butter with flour and slowly add this to the sauce. Mix well and add the mustard. Pour over baked lobsters and serve immediately.

Ragosta co la Panna
Lobster with Cream

1 large lobster, preboiled
3 tblspns butter
seasoning
1 cup thin cream
1 cup rice, boiled in water till *al dente* and kept warm
1 small onion, finely chopped
½ cup butter
3 tblspns grated Parmesan or other hard cheese
3 egg yolks
¼ cup Marsala, sweet sherry or port
2 tblspns butter
pinch of cayenne pepper or hot paprika

Remove meat from the tail and claws and slice thinly. Place meat in a pot with the butter and seasoning and brown slightly. Add cream, reduce heat and simmer till cream is reduced by half.

Sauté the onion in the butter till golden and add the warm rice and cheese, stirring well. Place rice on a serving dish and leave a well in the centre. Remove lobster from cream and place in the centre of the well, leaving the cream in the pot.

Add the eggs mixed with the wine to the cream and cook over low heat until slightly thickened. Add butter and cayenne pepper or paprika.

Pour sauce over the lobster meat and serve immediately.

Bacalà Mantecato
Salt Cod Mantecato

In Venice and the Veneto region there are two names for dried cod, *bacalà* which is salted and *stoccafisso* which is unsalted.

In north Europe cod used to be laid out for months on end to dry till it was as hard and stiff as the boards it was dried on. In southern Europe the process was helped by the sun and was much quicker – perhaps that's why the Venetians say 'stiff as a stockfish' and the English 'stiff as a board'! Because the Venetians had plentiful supplies of salt from Chioggia they could use this as well to help preserve the fish.

When using *bacalà*, it should be well pounded and then soaked overnight in cold – or even better, steadily running – water. Then remove the skin and clean the fish well. Fresh cod can also be used in this and the following three recipes.

At the Cipriani they add a little fresh cream to this recipe – Chef Renato Piccolotto's creation.

1lb 7oz/650g fresh or dried salt cod
olive oil
1 tblspn parsley, chopped
1 clove garlic, chopped
seasoning

If the fish is dried prepare as described above. Bring to boil in a pot of water and then remove pot from heat and leave fish to stand for 15–20 minutes in the hot water.

Remove, drain well and remove all the bones, skin etc. Flake flesh into tiny pieces. Place the fish in a deep dish and, adding a little oil at a time, beat with a wooden spoon – exactly as one would make mayonnaise. Continue thus, adding a little oil at a time and beating well, till mixture becomes white and creamy and the fish will not absorb any more oil. (This can also be done in a food processor.) Add the rest of the ingredients.

Serve with pieces of grilled yellow polenta.

Torcello

Bacalà a la Capussina
Salt Cod Capuchin

1lb 7oz/650g fresh or dried salt cod
2 tblspns olive oil
2 tblspns butter
1 clove garlic, chopped
1 tblspn chopped parsley
35fl oz/1 litre milk
1 tblspn currants or raisins
1 tblspn pinenuts
seasoning to taste

If using dried fish prepare as described above and then break fish into medium-sized pieces.

Sauté the garlic and parsley in the oil and butter till garlic is golden. Lower the heat and add the fish and seasoning. Stirring continuously, add a good quantity of milk and thereafter a little at a time. When the milk has almost all been reduced and the fish cooked, add the raisins and nuts.

Bacalà a la Vicentina
Salt Cod Vicentina

1lb 2oz/500g fresh or dried salt cod
9oz/260g olive oil
11fl oz/300ml milk
1 onion
1 tblspn parsley
2 tblspns flour
3 salted sardines or anchovies, boned
seasoning to taste

If using dried fish, prepare as described above.

Sauté the onion in the oil. When the onion is tender and pale in colour, add the parsley, flour, cod, anchovies or sardines, seasoning and milk. Mix well together and place in an ovenware dish. Place in a cool oven (300°F/150°C) and cook slowly, uncovered, till all the milk has been reduced (about 1 hour).

Serve with polenta.

Bacalà in Umido co la Uveta
Salt Cod Stewed with Raisins

1lb 7oz/650g fresh or dried salt cod
1 large onion, chopped
2 tblspns oil
½ cup tomato sauce (see Sauces)
1 cup water
pepper to taste
3 tblspns pinenuts
3 tblspns raisins, plumped in warm water

If using dried fish, prepare as described above.

Sauté the onion in the oil till transparent and tender. Add the tomato sauce mixed with the water. Leave to simmer till this slightly thickens.

Add the fish and rest of the ingredients and simmer for 20–30 minutes.

Bisato su le Bronze
Charcoal-grilled Eel

This a Chioggia island recipe and it is a traditional Christmas Eve dish. In fact, eel prepared most ways is traditional for Christmas Eve.

1 eel, rubbed all over with wood ash to remove slimyness and rinsed well
bayleaves, preferably fresh
seasoning to taste
skewers

Cut prepared eel into pieces roughly finger length. Put on to skewers, alternating with bayleaves. Season and grill over charcoal.

The eel is ready when the skin is crisp and dry. Eel is a very oily fish and does not need basting with any additional oil.

Bisato su l' Ara
Ara-cooked Eel

The *ara* is the cooling-down furnace for newly made glassware, although I really don't imagine anyone having one! This is another traditional Christmas Eve dish, this time from Murano island.

1 eel, rubbed and rinsed as above
5 fresh bayleaves
seasoning

Cut eel into pieces and place in an ovenware dish together with the bayleaves. Season. Place in a moderate oven and roast till done (about 25 minutes).

Island in the Lagoon

Bisato in Umido
Stewed Eel

Another Christmas Eve dish.

eel prepared as above and then marinaded in
water mixed with 1 tblspn vinegar
1 clove garlic, bruised
½ cup tomato sauce or tinned tomato purée
1 drop oil
1 bayleaf
seasoning to taste

Cut the eel into finger-length pieces. Sauté the garlic in just enough oil to brown. Add the rest of the ingredients to the pan and every now and then add a little hot water when necessary. Simmer the eel in the sauce till cooked. The sauce should not be too liquid.

Bisato Frito
Fried Eel

1 eel, prepared as above
1 lemon
flour
1 egg, beaten
enough breadcrumbs to coat eel
oil for frying
lemon wedges

Cut the eel into finger-length pieces and remove the spinal bone. Dry and dust pieces with flour and season well. Dip into the egg and then into the breadcrumbs, coating well.

Fry in hot oil till golden-brown. Serve with lemon wedges.

Branzin o Orada al Forno
Baked Bass or John Dory

1 bass or John Dory, approx 1¾lb/800g
4 tblspns butter
4 tblspns chopped parsley
seasoning to taste
juice of 1 lemon
½ cup white wine

Clean and scale the fish. In the dish in which the fish is to be baked, put half the butter and half the parsley, season, and place the fish on top. Sprinkle the fish with the rest of the butter and parsley and season once again. Bake in a moderate oven till nicely done (about 25 minutes).

Carefully remove the fish and place on a warm serving dish. Keep warm.

Meanwhile on top of the stove put the lemon juice and wine into the dish or pan where the fish was baked and deglaze.

Serve fish with sauce poured over.

Brusiolo (Sepia in Tecia)
Stewed Cuttlefish or Squid

This is a recipe from San Pietro in Volta, an island famous for its fish.

14oz/400g cuttlefish or squid
1 tblspn oil
1 piece fresh rosemary
1 onion, chopped
½ cup tomato sauce (*see* Sauces)
or tinned tomato purée
¼ cup water
seasoning to taste

Clean the squid or cuttlefish, remove the eyes, inksacs and cuttle or plastic-like backbone and cut into pieces. Put all the ingredients in a pan. Simmer, covered, for about 2½ hours or until tender. Serve with boiled rice.

For those who like piquant dishes, add some chilli, or any hot pepper.

Barboni (Triglie) in Salsa
Red Mullet in a Sharp Sauce

4 red mullets, cleaned and scaled
2 tblspns oil
juice of 1 lemon
½ cup white wine
seasoning
1 tblspn tomato sauce (*see* Sauces)
or tinned tomato purée
1 tspn made mustard

Place the fish in a pan with a lid. Sprinkle with oil, lemon, wine and seasoning and cover. Cook the fish by gently simmering over low heat or in a cool oven (275-300°F/140–150°C) for 15 minutes. Remove gently on to a warm serving dish and keep warm.

Add the remaining ingredients to the pan juices and simmer till sauce thickens. Serve with sauce poured over the fish.

This may also be eaten cold.

Botarga de Bosega
Mullet Roe Packed, Salted, and Dried

This was an old custom during the Serenissima Republic, which has now practically fallen into disuse. The eggs or roe of the mullet were salted and dried and tightly packed into long, thin, sausage-like shapes. These were expensive as many fish roes were needed. In Pelestrina and Chioggia there are still some old fishermen who keep up the tradition for their own personal use. In Sardinia and Sicily the tradition still exists but instead of mullet roe, tuna fish roe is used.

The *botarga* is sliced and served on bread and butter, or grated over spaghetti cooked *al dente* and tossed in butter or olive oil.

Caparozzoli (Tartufi di Mare) o Peoci o Vongole o Tutto Misto
Mussels or Clams or Mixed

Any type of bivalve shellfish may be used.

3lb 5oz/1½kg shellfish
1–2 tblspns oil
1 clove garlic, bruised
2 tblspns parsley, chopped
pepper to taste

Leave the shellfish in clean seawater for a few hours or overnight if possible, changing the water at least 3 times to get rid of the sand trapped inside them.

Heat the oil and add the garlic, pepper and parsley and add mussels or clams etc. Place well fitting lid on the pan and shake occasionally over very high heat in order to open up the mussels or clams etc. Remove all those which are open and reheat those which are still closed. (This could have been caused by the clams not being thoroughly heated through.) *Remove and discard* after this any which have not opened or may be broken.

Serve on a large serving plate or dish, fairly deep, with all the sauce poured over the clams etc. Serve with plenty of bread for dunking and finger bowls for washing the hands.

Canocie (Cicale di Mare)
Mantis Prawns

Mantis prawns are similar to tiger prawns.

24 mantis prawns
pot boiling water
salt
2 lemon halves
oil
2 tblspns parsley, chopped
pepper to taste

Place the mantis prawns in pot of boiling water and bring back to boil, timing 3 minutes from when they start to boil.

Take out and snip tails at an angle towards the centre thus forming a triangle. Cut away ¼in/½cm down both sides. Remove the top layer of outer shell (not the belly part) to expose the flesh.

Arrange on a dish and sprinkle with oil, parsley, lemon and pepper to taste.

Note: if these are cooked longer the flesh disintegrates and you find yourself with an empty carcass.

Canocie o Peoci Ripiene
Stuffed Mantis Prawns or Mussels

24 mantis prawns *or* 2lb 3oz/1kg mussels
1oz/25g salami or sopressa, finely chopped or minced
1 cup breadcrumbs
3 tblspns chopped parsley
juice of ½ lemon
1 egg, beaten
¼ cup Parmesan cheese, grated
seasoning to taste
oil

Boil and snip the prawns as described above and arrange on an ovenproof dish. If using the mussels place them in a hot oven for a few minutes till they open; debeard and keep on one half of their shell.

Mix together all the rest of the ingredients except the oil to form a stuffing and pack a little of the stuffing on top of each prawn or mussel. Add a drop or two of oil to prevent drying out.

Place under grill till golden. Serve hot or cold.

Cape Sante in Tecia
Pan-cooked Scallops with Sauce

This dish can also be served as an *antipasto*, using half the quantities.

16–24 scallops
2–3 tblspns oil
1 clove garlic, bruised
2 tblspns parsley, chopped
½ tblspn tomato sauce (*see* Sauces)
or tinned tomato purée

Place scallops in a large pan or in a hot oven on a baking sheet till they open. When the scallops open, they loose a little of their juice. Drain the juice off and mix together with the rest of the ingredients (except the scallops) and gently heat. Meanwhile, remove the beard and black intestine from the scallops and discard. Add the scallops to the sauce, and heat through.

Cape Sante co la Salsa de Fonghi
Scallops with a Mushroom Sauce

12 scallops
1 cup fairly thick béchamel sauce
1 cup cooked mushrooms
1 tblspn chopped parsley
2 tblspns red wine
seasoning
sweet paprika (optional)

Clean and open the scallops in a hot oven as described above. Debeard and remove intestines. Replace scallops in half their shell.

Add all the rest of the ingredients except the scallops to the béchamel in the pot and cook till alcohol in wine has evaporated. Pour a little over each scallop in its shell half. Place under hot grill till golden.

Decorate with a sprig of parsley and a sprinkle of paprika.

Cape Longhe Gratinae
Pencil Bait (Razor Clams) au Gratin

The Venetian name for these means 'long clams' or 'finger clams', because of the way they have to be pulled out of the sand. They are usually only used as bait in other countries.

2lb 3oz/1kg pencil bail
2 cloves garlic
1 tblspn chopped parsley
6 tblspns breadcrumbs
1 tblspn butter
lemon
oil
seasoning

Wash and open shells, removing the mollusc.

Sauté the breadcrumbs in the butter till golden, remove, place in a bowl and leave to cool. Add to these the garlic and parsley and a little oil to amalgamate it all and season to taste.

Replace the pencil bait in a shell half, and place in a long ovenproof dish. Place a little of the breadcrumb mixture on each pencil bait and pack well down. Then put a little oil on top of each to prevent drying out. Bake in hot oven till brown (about 15–20 minutes).

Serve with lemon squeezed over them.

Cape Longhe o Cape da Deo Lessi
Pencil Bait (Razor Clams)
Boiled and Dressed

It is said that Rossini composed the opening strains of *The Barber of Seville* after hearing the fishermen at the Rialto fishmarket shouting after bustling shoppers in their particular singsong way, 'Cape da deo, cape da deo'.

2lb 3oz/1kg pencil bait, cleaned and
left in salted water
3 tblspns butter
3 tblspns oil
1 tblspn chopped parsley
3 cloves garlic, bruised
lemon
seasoning

Heat the butter and oil together in a large pan and gently sauté the garlic till golden. Remove and discard. Add the parsley. Increase the heat and add the pencil bait and cook for 10 minutes more till the shells open. These, as they open, throw out their own liquid which, together with the other ingredients in the pan, makes a delicious sauce.

Serve bait removed from their shells with the sauce poured over and a squeeze of lemon juice. Serve with plenty of toast or French bread.

Canestrei (Ostreche Pettini)
Miniature (Queen or Bay) Scallops

These are usually sold without shells. Cook as for pencil bait. These are included in the classic *Frittura mista* (*see* below).

Coe de Rospo Impanae
Crumbed Angler Fish or Monkfish

4 small (1¾lb/800g) angler fish or monkfish, skinned
with head removed
½ tblspn butter
1½ cups breadcrumbs mixed with salt and pepper and
a good pinch of nutmeg
1–2 eggs
butter for frying
lemon wedges

Poach the monkfish for 10–15 minutes in 1 pint/½ litre water with the ½ tblspn butter and some salt. This gets rid of their excess liquid. Remove fish, drain well, split down the middle and remove backbone without cutting right through the two halves, as these must remain joined.

Dip fish in some flour and then in the beaten egg and next into the breadcrumbs. Fry gently in plenty of butter and serve with lemon wedges.

Calamaretti Friti
Fried Small Squid

1¾lb/800g tiny squids, cleaned, with mouths, eyes and sacs removed
flour for dusting
oil for frying
seasoning
lemon wedges

Dust with the flour and fry in hot oil. Remove and drain when nicely golden. Season and serve with lemon wedges.

Calamaretti a la Graela
Grilled Small Squid

1¾lb/800g tiny squids, cleaned as above
olive oil
1 tblspn chopped parsley
seasoning

Cook in oven or on top of stove or better still barbeque the squids and brush with oil every now and then to prevent them from sticking; these only take a very short while to cook so take care not to over cook as they become tough.

Serve with an oil, parsley and seasoning dressing.

Campo San Pantalon - Rio Foscari

Calamaretti Lessi
Boiled Squid

1¾lb/800g squids, slightly larger than for the other
recipes, cleaned as above
1 clove garlic, chopped
1 tblspn chopped parsley
lemon juice
olive oil
seasoning

Bring to boil a pot of salted water. Spear a squid on to a fork and dip into the boiling water slowly. This allows the tentacles to curl and forms a flower-like shape. Remove and cool while repeating the same procedure with all the squids. This procedure is repeated three times for each squid till the squid become tender and white. The reason for this time consuming method is that it prevents the squids from over cooking and thus becoming tough.

Remove and drain well and serve with dressing made of the remaining ingredients.

Calamaretti col Pien
Stuffed Squid

1¾lb/800g fairly small squids, cleaned as above
1 clove garlic
1 tblspn parsley
½ cup breadcrumbs
1 tblspn white wine
oil
seasoning

Remove the tentacles from the body and thoroughly clean the body under water. Remove the mouth and eyes from the tentacles and finely chop or mince tentacles together with the garlic, parsley, breadcrumbs, seasoning and enough oil to bind the mixture. Fill the squid heads with this and close with a toothpick. Place in an oiled ovenware dish and sprinkle a little oil and wine over each one.

Season and bake in a moderate oven for about 45 minutes.

Calamari in Umido
Stewed Squid

1¾lb/800g squid, cleaned as above and
sliced into rings and pieces
3 tblspns oil (approx)
1½lb/700g peeled tomatoes, sieved
2 cloves garlic
1 tblspn chopped parsley
3 tblspns white wine
1oz/30g capers

seasoning
paprika (optional)
3½oz/100g green olives (optional)

Heat approx 3 tblspns oil in a pan, preferably earthenware, and sauté the garlic and parsley adding a little wine at a time and allowing the wine to evaporate almost completely every time. Add the squid pieces, sieved tomatoes, capers and optional olives and paprika. Season to taste. Add a little hot water and cover the casserole and gently simmer for about one hour. Add more water if necessary.

Serve with new boiled potatoes, plain or dressed with oil, garlic and chopped parsley.

Folpi in Tecia
Pan-cooked Octopus or Seacat

If octopus is not available use large squid.

2lb 3oz/1kg cleaned octopi each weighing not more
than 7oz/200g
2 onions, chopped
3 tblspns oil
3 tblspns butter
1 pinch nutmeg
2 bayleaves
1 tblspn tomato concentrate
1 glass red wine
seasoning
3 potatoes, diced (optional)

Sauté gently the sliced octopi in the oil and butter. Add onions, optional potatoes, seasoning, nutmeg and bayleaves. Cover and gently cook for ½ hour.

Add the wine and cook, uncovered, till it has evaporated. Add the tomato diluted with a little hot water. Cover with lid once again and simmer gently till the octopi are tender.

Squero di San Trovaso

Sally Spector 1982

Garusoli
Seasnails

One can use any type of whelk or seasnail (so long as they are edible!). Periwinkles may be used as well.

4lb 6oz/2kg seasnails
1 piece lemon peel
3 tblspns vinegar
1 tblspn chopped parsley
oil
seasoning

Wash the seasnails well. Place in a pot of salted water, together with lemon peel and vinegar and gently simmer for about 45 minutes or until tender. Remove from their shells with a toothpick or pin.
 Serve cold with a dressing of oil, parsley, seasoning, and hot polenta.

Garusoli in Umido
Stewed Seasnails

Whelks can also be used.

4lb 6oz/2kg seasnails
1 piece lemon peel
3 tblspns vinegar
3 tblspns oil
2 large onions, diced
1 tblspn rosemary leaves
1 clove garlic
1 cup tomatoes, peeled and sieved
paprika (optional)

Prepare and simmer seasnails as for the previous recipe and remove from shells. Sauté the onions in the oil, add the rosemary, minced, and the garlic. When the onions are tender, add the seasnails, tomato, optional paprika and a little water.
 Simmer all together till tender, adding a little at a time some water if necessary.
 Serve with polenta.

Fortagia de Gambareti
Shrimp Omelette

This is traditionally served around Christmas.

6 eggs
seasoning
1–2 tblspns water
1 pat of butter
250g peeled, precooked shrimps

Beat eggs together with the water and seasoning. Heat the butter in the pan and pour the egg mixture into the pan. Add the shrimps and cook till nicely done, about 6 minutes.
 Serve with a salad.

Frittura Mista
Mixed Fried Fish and Shellfish

1¾–2¼lb/800g–1kg mixed fish and shellfish, eg squid rings, scampi, shrimps, whitebait, small pieces of sole, sardines, pieces of eel and any type of mussel (these must be cleaned, shelled, boned, skinned, washed and dried)
2 cups (approx) flour
oil for frying
salt
lemon wedges

Prepare all the fish and shellfish so it is ready to be fried. Toss and coat very well in the flour. Heat the oil in a pot with frying basket. When the oil is hot put in the fish in the following order: squid rings, pieces of octopus, then the mussels and then the scampi, shrimps and sole and then the rest of the little fish. If using eel put in together with the scampi. When they all start rising to the top they should be golden in colour.
 Remove from the oil and drain well. Salt and serve with lemon wedges and a salad.
 Note: if your frying container is not big enough to take this amount of mixed fish, fry in two lots, as too many fish in too little oil lowers the heat of the oil and results in soggy fish.

Gambari o Gambareti Lessi
Dressed Prawns or Shrimps

2lb 3oz/1kg prawns or shrimps
4 cups water
½ tspn salt
1 tblspn vinegar
1 finger-length sprig rosemary
4 peppercorns
4 basil leaves
2 tblspns chopped parsley

for dressing:
oil
lemon juice
seasoning
1 clove garlic (optional)

Wash the shrimps or prawns. Place the rest of the ingredients in a pot and when just starting to boil, drop the shrimps or prawns in, and simmer for 3-5 minutes. Take out, shell and remove vein down back.
 Dress with oil and lemon juice and seasoning with or without a clove of garlic added or with the Venetian 'Green Sauce' (*see* Sauces).

Gambaroni in Graela (Masanete)
Grilled Prawns

32 large prawns
32 sage leaves
6 tblspns breadcrumbs
32 pieces thinly sliced fat ham
seasoning
lemon

Wash prawns and peel. Wrap a piece of ham around each and place on skewers, alternating with a sage leaf (8 shrimps per person).
 Grill, and when ham starts to sizzle, remove skewers, roll them in the breadcrumbs and replace under the grill till golden.
 Serve with lemon juice squeezed over.

Granceole Gratinae
Crabs au Gratin

4 crabs (preferably 2 male and 2 female – the male has
less meat), soaked in fresh water (*see* below)
1 egg yolk
2 tblspns chopped parsley
9oz/250g single cream
breadcrumbs
seasoning

Place crabs in salted boiling water, cover, and
simmer for a maximum of 10 minutes. Remove
and drain.

When cool, remove the flesh, coral and leg
flesh and place in a bowl. Mince or finely flake
this together with the egg, parsley, cream and
seasoning. Mix well.

Return mixture to the shells, sprinkle with
breadcrumbs and bake in hot oven till golden,
about 10 minutes.

Granceola co la Salsa
Crab with a Sharp Sauce

4 crabs (as previous recipe)
2 carrots
1 stalk celery
2 bayleaves
2 tblspns lemon juice
2 hardboiled eggs
1 tblspn premade mustard
oil
seasoning
lemon juice

Boil crabs for 10 minutes with the carrots, celery,
bayleaves and lemon juice. Remove and drain.
Remove the flesh from the body, putting aside
the 'creamy' part and the coral. Remove the flesh
from the legs. Dice the firm flesh and replace in
the shells.

Then cream together the 'creamy' flesh, coral,
eggs and mustard, adding a little oil at a time to
make a creamy sauce. Add lemon juice to taste
and seasoning and serve in sauce boat.

Moleche a la Venezziana
Venetian Shore Crabs

This recipe and the following use shore crabs
which have just lost their hard outer shell. These
crustaceans lose their outer shell twice a year, in
spring and autumn. They are therefore
completely tender and edible in a crunchy way. I
should think that taking this creature in its
vulnerable state is prohibited in most other
countries but in Venice it is considered a
delicacy and is actually cultivated in enormous
quantities.

2lb 3oz/1kg shore crabs, without hard outer shell
flour
oil
seasoning

In Venice these poor creatures are usually fried
alive but I do not go along with this type of
torture if it can be helped and so I place them in
fresh water for a few hours till they lose
consciousness as it's much kinder.

Remove the ends of the claws, dust crabs with
flour and fry in hot oil and drain well. Season.

Moleche a la Muranese
Murano Island Shore Crabs

2lb 3oz/1kg shore crabs, without hard outer shells
2 eggs, well beaten
flour
oil
seasoning

Place the live crabs in the beaten egg and leave
till they have absorbed the egg and suffocated.
Flour them well and fry in hot oil. Season

Sardele o Sfogi in Saor
Soused or Pickled Sardines or Sole

This is a fourteenth-century recipe. The dish is
traditional on Redeemer Day (Redentore), the
third Sunday in July.

2lb 3oz/1kg sardines or fillets of sole
flour *or* maizemeal for dusting
oil
9fl oz/¼ litre vinegar
9fl oz/¼ litre white wine
1 tblspn sugar (optional)
1oz/30g pinenuts
1oz/30g raisins, soaked in tepid water
seasoning
2 large onions, thinly sliced

Clean fish and remove heads, and insides at the
same time if using sardines.

Dust the fish with flour and gently sauté in a
little hot oil till golden. Remove and drain and
place in an earthenware dish.

Meanwhile sauté onions in the same oil till
tender, then add the rest of the ingredients and
boil for 3 minutes. Pour over the fish and leave it
all to stand till cool.

This may be stored for a long time in the
refrigerator.

Cisame de Pesse
Soused Sole or Sardines

This is a recipe from the 1300s. Mackerel can
also be used in this way.

2lb 3oz/1kg whole sole, skin and fins removed or
whole sardines, head and fins removed
2 large onions, sliced thinly
1 tblspn oil
2oz/50g butter

milk and cornmeal or flour for coating
oil
2½–4fl oz/75–125ml vinegar
9fl oz/425ml water
1 tspn honey
2 tblspns blanched, halved almonds
2 tblspns raisins
pinch each powdered cloves, cayenne and nutmeg
salt and pepper

Gently sauté the onions in the oil and butter until softened but not coloured, adding a little water if necessary. Dip the fish in the milk and then in the cornmeal or flour to coat. Fry in hot oil until cooked and golden-brown. Remove and keep warm.

Add the rest of the ingredients except the fish to the onions and simmer, uncovered, for 10–15 minutes. Pour the sauce over the fish and cool. Keep in refrigerator, removing 15 minutes before serving.

This will keep in refrigerator for a week.

Pesse al Marsala
Fish Fillets with Marsala

1lb 5oz/600g firm-flesh fish fillets
2 tblspns oil
flour for dusting
1 tblspn minced parsley or
basil or half and half
1 onion, chopped
seasoning
juice of 1 lemon
½ cup Marsala

Rialto Market

Gently sauté the floured fish in oil in a pan together with the herbs, onion and seasoning. When the fish is cooked through on both sides, sprinkle lemon juice over the fish and continue cooking over low heat for a few minutes. Add the Marsala and simmer till it slowly evaporates. This makes a fairly thick sauce.

Peoci Fritti
Fried Mussels

2lb 3oz/1kg mussels
flour
2 eggs, beaten
seasoning
pinch nutmeg
oil
breadcrumbs
lemon wedges
2 tblspns chopped parsley

Scrub shells clean. To open place on a baking tray in oven and remove immediately they open. *Discard any which do not open.* Debeard and remove the mussels from their shells. Dust with flour. Dip into beaten egg, which has been seasoned and with nutmeg added. Roll in breadcrumbs, coating well. Fry in hot oil on both sides till golden.

Serve with lemon wedges and parsley.

Rane Frite
Fried Frogs

24 frogs, cleaned and ready for cooking
flour
oil
seasoning
lemon wedges
parsley sprigs

Wash and dry the frogs well and dust with flour. Shake off excess flour. Fry in hot oil on both sides till golden.

Serve with lemon wedges and decorate with parsley.

Sarde a 'Scotadeo'
'Burnt Fingers' Sardines

With this recipe you can also use grey or red mullet or any other type of fish, cut into pieces.

16–20 whole sardines, the larger the better
4-5 tblspns oil
seasoning
lemon juice (optional)

Place the cleaned, gutted and scaled fish in an earthenware dish and toss in the oil, seasoning and optional lemon juice. Leave for about 2 hours.

Remove fish and season once again and grill.

Serve each piece in a paper serviette. Serve very hot.

Sardele col Parsemolo
Sardines with Parsley

16-20 large sardines
3 tblspns water
oil
seasoning
1 tblspn parsley
juice of 1 lemon
2 cloves garlic, finely chopped

Remove sardine heads and intestines and wash, scale and then dry the fish well.

Place in a pan with a drop of oil on each and add the water, seasoning and parsley. Cover and gently simmer for 10–15 minutes. Remove lid and cook till all liquid has evaporated. Sprinkle the lemon juice over the fish and cook for a further 10 minutes.

Sprinkle the garlic over and leave to cool.

Sardele 'Incinte' o 'In Stato'
Pregnant Sardines

What is really meant is 'stuffed' so don't be alarmed!

2lb 3oz/1kg sardines, as large as possible
bayleaves
vinegar
1 cup breadcrumbs
2 tblspns pinenuts
2 tblspns parsley
1 tblspn sultanas
juice 1 orange
oil
seasoning
1 cup white wine
lemon juice

Scale fish and remove heads, intestines and backbones. The fish is then a nice flat fillet. Sprinkle with a little vinegar and bayleaves and leave to stand for a few minutes. Dry well.

Make the stuffing by mincing the breadcrumbs, most of the pinenuts, parsley and most of the sultanas together. Add the orange juice, seasoning and enough oil to make a fairly stiff stuffing. Add more breadcrumbs if necessary.

Spread a little of this on each fillet and then place two fillets together, thus making a little sandwich of fish with the stuffing in the middle.

Place in an ovenware dish and sprinkle with the wine and a little oil and lemon juice. Sprinkle rest of pinenuts and sultanas over the fish and bake in hot oven for 5 minutes covered and another 5 minutes uncovered.

Sardele Impanae
Sardines Fried in Batter

2lb 3oz/1kg sardines
flour
2 eggs, beaten
seasoning
pinch of nutmeg
oil
lemon wedges

Season and put a pinch of nutmeg in the beaten eggs. Clean and prepare the fish into fillets as for the previous recipe. Dust with flour and dip into the egg. Fry in hot oil till golden on both sides.

Drain on absorbent paper and serve with lemon wedges.

Scampi Friti
Fried Scampi

Either cook these as for the 'Fritura Mista' (*see above*) or floured, dipped into seasoned beaten egg, and then fried in hot oil.

Scampi a la Graela
Grilled Scampi

20 scampi
oil
seasoning
2 cloves garlic
3 tblspns parsley
fresh oil for dressing

Cut down along the back in the centre of the scampi with a sharp pair of scissors, but not actually cutting the scampi into two. Baste with a little oil and season. Grill, preferably over live coals – if scampi are placed on skewers this is easier to do. When the slit along the back starts widening and opening up, it signifies the scampi are cooked to perfection.

Place on a serving dish and dress with fresh oil, and mixed minced garlic and parsley.

Sfogi Fritti
Fried Sole

4 sole fillets
flour
2 eggs, beaten
pinch nutmeg
2 tblspns Parmesan cheese
breadcrumbs
seasoning
oil
lemon wedges

Mix eggs, nutmeg and cheese. Dry the fillets and dust with flour. Dip into the beaten egg mixture and then coat well with breadcrumbs. Fry in hot oil till golden on both sides. Season.

Serve with lemon wedges.

Sfogi in Vin Bianco
Sole in White Wine

1¾lb/800g sole fillets
seasoning
1 scallion
¼ cup butter, melted
½ cup dry white wine
1 tblspn chopped parsley
½ tspn thyme
2 bayleaves, crushed
1 tblspn butter
1½ tspns flour
2 tblspns single cream
1 tblspn butter
parsley sprigs

Butter a baking dish well. (This must have a lid.) Place the fillets in a single layer and sprinkle with salt, pepper, chopped scallion, melted butter, wine, parsley, thyme and bayleaves. Put the lid on the dish after having covered the dish with greaseproof paper. Bake in moderate oven for about 20 minutes.

Remove fillets and pour the juices from the baking dish into a small pot. Add the tblspn butter and allow to melt. Blend in the flour and add the cream and cook for a couple of minutes. Pour this sauce over the fish and serve with parsley sprigs as decoration.

Sepe in Umido col Tocio Rosso
Cuttlefish Stewed in a Red Sauce

1¾lb/800g cuttlefish
½ cup oil
1 clove garlic
2 tblspns chopped parsley
2 bayleaves
2 pieces lemon peel
seasoning
1 cup water
2 tblspns tomato concentrate
2 tblspns Marsala

Clean the cuttlefish, removing the eyes, mouth and inksacs. Cut into slices.

Sauté the garlic and parsley in oil till golden and then remove and discard garlic.

Add the cuttlefish, seasoning, bayleaves and lemon peel. Simmer for 5 minutes. Add the tomato concentrate diluted with the water and Marsala. Simmer till the sauce has been reduced and the cuttlefish is tender. Add water if necessary. The sauce should be fairly thick.

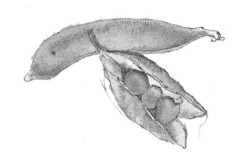

Sepe coi Bisi
Cuttlefish with Peas

1¾lb/800g cuttlefish
2 tblspns oil
2 cloves garlic
3 tblspns chopped parsley
seasoning
½ cup white wine
3½oz/100g fatty ham or bacon, diced
9oz/250g fresh or frozen peas
1 tblspn brandy

Clean cuttlefish as described above and slice into pieces. Heat most of oil and sauté the cuttlefish, garlic and parsley together till the garlic is golden. Remove and discard the garlic. Add the seasoning, wine and from time to time add a little hot water till the cuttlefish is tender.

Meanwhile gently sauté the ham or bacon in a little oil and add the peas and simmer for 15 minutes till tender. After 10 minutes add the brandy. Add ham and pea mixture to the cuttlefish and heat together thoroughly

Sepe col Pien
Stuffed Cuttlefish

8 small cuttlefish
1 egg
4 tblspns cheese, Parmesan if possible
2 slices bread, soaked in milk
2 tblspns parsley, chopped
2 cloves garlic
4 tomatoes peeled and chopped
or a small tin of peeled tomatoes
1 cup white wine
seasoning
oregano
oil

Clean and remove eyes, mouth and inksacs and wash well. Remove the tentacles and head, leaving body. Mince together the tentacles and head, squeezed out bread, parsley and garlic. Add the cheese, beaten egg and seasoning, mixing well. Fill the bodies with the mixture ensuring that they are not over filled as the stuffing increases as it cooks. Close the body with a toothpick or sew closed.

Then sauté the stuffed cuttlefish on both sides in a little oil for a few minutes. Add the wine and simmer for 3 minutes. Add tomatoes and seasoning. Place in a moderate oven for ½ hour or till they are tender.

Place in a serving dish and remove toothpicks or thread. Sprinkle with a *little* oregano and pour the sauce over.

Schille Frite
Fried Grey Shrimps

These are cooked as in the recipe for Frittura Mista. The shells are left on.

Sievolo in Graela
Grilled Mullet

4 mullet (approx 7oz/200g each)
2 cloves garlic
2 sprigs marjoram
1 tblspn oil
1 tspn vinegar
juice 1 lemon
seasoning

Clean, scale and remove intestines of the fish. Make diagonal incisions along the length of the fish. Place the fish in a dish and sprinkle with a little oil and the lemon juice. Season and leave for 1 hour.

Meanwhile mince the garlic and marjoram together using oil and vinegar to make a little basting liquid to baste the fish from time to time. Grill the fish over hot coals or grid pan basting from time to time with the above sauce. Do not turn the fish over.

Serve with the sauce which is left over.

Ton Fresco in Tecia
Pan-cooked Fresh Tuna

1¾lb/800g fresh tuna slices
2 large onions, chopped
2 tblspns oil
2 tblspns butter
3 salted sardines
flour
3 peeled tomatoes, chopped
or a small tin peeled tomatoes
1 cup white wine

Heat oil and butter and sauté the onions till tender and golden. Flour the tuna and sauté this till golden on both sides. Add the rest of the ingredients and cook over low heat till done.

Trota a la Venessiana
Venetian Trout

4 small trout
4 tblspns butter
8 sage leaves
4 tblspns parsley
white *or* red wine to cover
seasoning
brandy

Clean, scale and remove the intestines from the fish. Mince the sage and parsley together and mix with the butter. Stuff the trout stomach-opening with this and close with a toothpick. Place in an ovenware dish and cover with the wine and season.

Bake in a moderate oven till cooked through. Pour over a little heated brandy and set alight. Serve immediately.

Ruga dei Speziali - bean and spice shop

6 VERDURE

VEGETABLES

Fondi o Cuori de Articiochi Friti
Fried Artichoke Bases or Hearts

12 small artichoke bases or hearts (*see* Antipasti)
2 eggs, beaten
flour
1 cup breadcrumbs
2 tblspns Parmesan cheese
seasoning
oil for frying

Half cook the artichoke bases or hearts in salted boiling water with a little lemon juice to prevent discolouring for 8–10 minutes, remove and allow to cool.

Season beaten eggs and mix the cheese with the breadcrumbs. Lightly flour the artichokes and then dip them into the egg and then coat well with the breadcrumb mixture.

Fry in hot oil till golden on both sides.

Articiochi coi Bisi
Artichokes with Peas

12 small artichoke bases or hearts
juice 1 lemon
2 tblspns oil
1 tblspn butter
7–9oz/200–250g fresh or frozen peas

Parboil the bases or hearts in salted water and a squeeze of lemon juice, till tender. Remove and drain.

Meanwhile, heat oil and butter and gently sauté the peas, parsley and garlic. Discard the garlic when it turns golden-brown. If, while cooking the peas, the liquid is too quickly absorbed add hot water a little at a time to prevent sticking. Add seasoning and when the peas are tender, add the artichokes and cook together for a further 5 minutes.

Castraure Lesse
Very Small Artichokes, Boiled

These artichokes are picked from the plant when they are slightly thicker than a thumb.

12 small artichokes
lemon juice
2 tblspns chopped parsley
oil
vinegar (optional)
seasoning

Fruit and Vegetable Boat at San Barnaba

Precook the artichokes in salted water, with lemon juice added, till tender. Remove and drain. Place in a serving dish and dress with the oil and optional vinegar and sprinkle with the parsley. Leave to stand till cool.

Sparesi Lessi
Boiled and Dressed Asparagus

1lb 2oz/½kg asparagus
seasoning
½ cup melted butter

Boil the asparagus in salted water, tied together in a bunch, in a deep pot so that the water will just cover the tips. The spears must remain upright. Do not let the salted water boil too fiercely.

The asparagus are done if the base of the stem when pierced is tender, but take care not to overcook as you could lose the lovely tender tip.

Remove carefully, untie and dress with melted butter.

Sparesi coi Vovi
Asparagus with Eggs

1lb 2oz/½kg asparagus
4 eggs
seasoning

Precook the asparagus as described above. Remove, drain and arrange on 4 plates with tips all in the same direction. Softboil the eggs till whites have set but the yolk still fairly runny. Peel and cut in half. Season. Each person takes an asparagus spear and dips it into the egg yolk.

Serve with finger bowls.

Fenoci in Tecia
Pan-cooked Fennel

8 fennel, cleaned and cut into quarters
lemon peel
1 cup stock
1 cup white wine
1 tblspn vinegar
1 bayleaf
seasoning
3 tblspns oil

Precook the fennel in salted water till tender. Remove and drain. Place in a casserole and add the rest of the ingredients and gently simmer for 30–40 minutes or until tender and very little liquid remains.

Fenoci col Late
Fennel cooked in Milk

8 very small fennel, quartered
2 tblspns butter
seasoning
1 cup milk
½ cup grated cheese

Melt butter in pan and add fennel. Season and sauté for a few minutes till golden-brown on each side. Lower heat and add milk.

Simmer gently till milk has almost evaporated and fennel are tender. Sprinkle the cheese on top.

Fonghi in Tecia
Pan-cooked Mushrooms

1lb 2oz/500g mushrooms (any type)
1 onion, chopped
1 clove garlic
2 tblspns chopped parsley
seasoning
1 tblspn oil

Clean and slice the mushrooms; dry well. Heat the oil and sauté the garlic, onion and parsley. When the garlic becomes golden, discard. Add the mushrooms and cook covered, stirring occasionally till the mushrooms are tender.

Season and add a little stock if all the liquid has been consumed, and it seems too dry. (The mushrooms will release their own juices while cooking.)

Serve with polenta or as a side dish.

Fonghi Trifolai
Truffled Mushrooms

1lb 2oz/500g mushrooms
1 tblspn oil
1 clove garlic
salt
2 tblspns chopped parsley
2 tblspns butter
seasoning
1 tblspn brandy

Heat the oil and sauté the sliced mushrooms, garlic and parsley with some salt. The mushrooms will lose water and so continue to gently cook these till all the liquid has been consumed. Add the butter and adjust the seasoning. Add the brandy and cook for 3–4 minutes more.

These are often eaten with polenta. In a greased mould, place a layer of cooked polenta and then all the truffled mushrooms and then fill the rest of the mould with more polenta. Leave to cool slightly and unmould.

Fasioi Sofegai
Suffocated (Stewed) Kidney Beans

9oz/250g prepared weight fresh, frozen or dried kidney beans
2 carrots, finely chopped
1 stalk celery, chopped
1 onion, chopped
1 sprig rosemary leaves, minced
2–3 tblspns oil
seasoning

If using dried beans, soak overnight.

Heat the oil and add the vegetables and rosemary and sauté till almost golden. Add the beans and a little hot water to cover and cover pot. Simmer over very low heat. Add a little water from time to time to keep beans covered.

When the beans are tender (about 1½–2 hours), season. Remove lid from pot and cook till liquid has evaporated.

Serve as it is or dressed with oil and vinegar.

Fasioi Bianchi Consi
Dressed Butter Beans

9oz/250g dried large white beans
1 onion
1 large tin peeled tomatoes, chopped
2 cloves garlic, chopped
seasoning
3 tblspns oil
vinegar
olive oil for dressing

Soak dried beans overnight.

Rinse beans well and place in a pot of cold water and bring to boil. When foam forms on top, remove, strain and rinse the beans under cold water once again.

Sauté the chopped onion in 3 tblspns oil till tender; add the tomatoes and garlic and the beans. Add enough water to cover, keeping a pot of hot water to add to the beans from time to time. Bring to the boil and then reduce the heat and simmer, covered, till the beans are tender. Add seasoning only when tender and all liquid has been consumed (about 1½–2 hours).

Remove from heat, and pour into a serving bowl and dress with olive oil and vinegar while still hot. Adjust seasoning. When cool add more dressing if needed.

Melanzane in Tecia
Aubergines cooked with Tomatoes

2 large aubergines
1 small tin peeled tomatoes
2 cloves garlic
1 tblspn vinegar
3 tblspns oil
seasoning
pinch of oregano

The habit here in Venice is to peel the aubergine using the peel for 'Melanzane al funghetto' (see below) and using the inside pulp for this recipe. This is not necessary as this recipe is just as good made with skin and pulp.

Dice the aubergine, salt it, and leave to drain at an angle.

Heat the oil and add the garlic, aubergine and seasoning and cook for 20 minutes. Add the tomatoes and oregano and cook for 10–15 minutes more.

Melanzane Trifolate (o al Funghetto)
Truffled (or Mushroom Style) Aubergines

If this is to be used as an *antipasto* serve with cantaloup melon slices.

2 large aubergines (long in shape not round)
3 tblspns oil
2 cloves garlic
3 tblspns chopped parsley

Remove the pulp and seeds, and cut the skin part into strips (about ½in/1cm wide). Salt strips and leave to drain.

Meanwhile sauté the parsley and garlic in the oil and remove and discard the garlic when golden. Add the aubergine and gently cook till all its liquid is consumed and it becomes tender and dark and shiny, similar to cooked mushrooms (about 20 minutes). Serve with beef or game.

Melanzane col Pien 1
Stuffed Aubergines 1

The stuffing in both this recipe and the next one can also be used for tomatoes – follow the method given for 'Tomatoes with stuffing' in Chapter 2.

2 aubergines
1 cup breadcrumbs
¼ cup grated Parmesan or any hard cheese
3 tblspns chopped parsley
2 cloves garlic, chopped
oil for frying
olive oil to amalgamate
seasoning
butter

Cut aubergines into rounds, about ½in/1cm thick, salt and leave to drain.

Mix rest of ingredients, together with a little olive oil, to form a fairly stiff but workable filling. Sauté the aubergine in the oil and remove. Place in an ovenware dish and on top of each place a little of the filling. Dot with butter and bake in moderate oven till golden-brown.

Melanzane col Pien 2
Stuffed Aubergines 2

2 aubergines
½ cup breadcrumbs
1 egg, beaten
2oz/50g ham or any leftover meat
1–2 tblspns tomato sauce (*see* Sauces)
2 tblspns chopped parsley
2 cloves garlic, minced
3 tblspns Parmesan cheese
oil (if necessary)

Prepare the aubergines as above. Mince or chop the meat, parsley and garlic together and add breadcrumbs, egg, cheese and tomato and mix well into a stiff but workable filling – add more breadcrumbs or some oil, whichever, to achieve this.

Place a little on each piece of aubergine and bake in moderate oven till golden-brown.

Campo dei Mori

Puré de Patate
Creamed Potatoes

You may well ask why I have included creamed (or mashed, as many say) potatoes. The reason is that most people haven't discovered that after the potatoes have been boiled *in* their jackets, which makes all the difference to the taste, and after the potatoes have been sieved or mashed, they are then returned to the pot on the stove over a low heat and creamed with the milk and butter and the end result is well worth all the effort! The taste and texture is unbeatable!

4 large *old* potatoes
½ cup *hot* milk
2–3 tblspns butter
seasoning
pinch nutmeg
and/or 1 tblspn grated cheese

Wash and scrub the potatoes well and boil them in their jackets in salted water till tender. Drain and remove skins.

Mash or sieve and then replace in the pot over low heat together with the hot milk and butter and stir, with a wooden spoon, constantly.

Test for seasoning and add nutmeg and/or cheese. The potatoes should be lovely and creamy.

Patate a la Venessiana
Venetian Potatoes

4 large potatoes
1 large onion, chopped
3 tblspns oil
3 tblspns butter
3 tblspns chopped parsley
seasoning
1 garlic clove, bruised (optional)

Peel and cut each potato into 8 pieces. Heat oil and butter and sauté onion till tender. Add the potatoes and gently cook till tender, stirring often. A bruised garlic clove may be added if wished.

When the potatoes are tender season and sprinkle with the parsley and serve hot.

Torta de Patate
Potato Pie

2lb 3oz/1kg potatoes
butter
seasoning
milk

Peel and slice potatoes very thinly – they should be transparent. In a greased ovenware dish, not too wide (about 8in/20cm in diameter), put a layer of potatoes and seasoning and dot with butter. Repeat till all the potatoes have been used.

Fill with enough milk to just cover the potatoes and bake in moderate oven until all the milk has been consumed and the potatoes are tender and done.

Polpete de Patate
Potato Croquettes

1 cup thick béchamel sauce
1lb 2oz/½kg boiled, peeled and mashed potatoes
3 tblspns grated cheese
2 eggs, beaten
seasoning
good pinch nutmeg
breadcrumbs
oil for frying

In a pot over a low heat stir the sauce and the potatoes together till well mixed. Remove from the heat and place in a bowl and add the cheese, eggs, seasoning and nutmeg to taste and mix well.

Form into finger lengths and roll in the breadcrumbs. Fry in the hot oil till golden all over.

Radicio de Treviso su la Graela
Grilled Treviso Salad Heads

These are a type of chicory with long red and white salad heads on the bitter side, but very tasty. I have used this recipe with endives and normal salad, quartered, with equal success.

4 small heads of salad
seasoning
oil

Clean and halve heads lengthwise, leaving roots on to facilitate turning the vegetable over while grilling. Dip in salted water. Grill on both sides. Dress with oil and season.

Radicio de Treviso al Butiro
Treviso Salad with Butter

4 small heads of salad
2 tblspns butter
seasoning

Cut heads into half or quarters depending on size. Place in a greased ovenware dish, dot with the butter and season. Bake in a moderate oven till tender.

Suca Baruca frita a la Venessiana
Venetian Fried Pumpkin

Courgettes, thinly sliced lengthwise, can also be used in this way.

1lb 2oz/½kg pumpkin
thick batter made with flour, water, salt, egg white
and pinch baking powder
oil for frying
seasoning

Peel, remove seeds and cut the pumpkin into equal pieces. Dip into the batter and fry in the hot oil till tender. Season. This is usually served with pork.

Fiori de Suca Friti
Fried Pumpkin or Courgette Flowers

These are delicious and are a must to try. Miniature courgettes with flowers still attached can also be used, cut in half first. Use a thick batter as above and fry in hot oil.

View from the Ponte dell'Olio

Suca Frita
Fried Pumpkin

1lb 2oz/½kg pumpkin
2 cloves garlic
½ cup olive oil
seasoning
1 sprig rosemary leaves, minced

Heat oil in a pan and put the garlic in and sauté till browned. Remove the garlic and discard. Add the pumpkin, cut into pieces, seasoning and minced rosemary and gently cook for 20 minutes. Stir often.

Suchete in Tecia
Pan-cooked Courgettes

1lb 2oz/½kg courgettes
3 tblspns chopped parsley
¼ cup oil
2 cloves garlic, chopped
seasoning
stock (if necessary)

Wash courgettes and cut in half lengthwise and then cut each half into small pieces. Sauté the parsley and garlic in the olive oil for 2 minutes. Add the courgettes and gently cook for 20–30 minutes. Add some hot stock if necessary to prevent from sticking.

Raise de Seano de Verona in Salsa
Celery in a Sauce

We use celery grown in Romeo and Juliet area, Verona.

1 large bunch celery
4 tblspns oil
2oz/50g bacon, diced
1 onion, chopped
seasoning
2oz/50g chopped mushrooms (optional)
2 tblspns tomato concentrate
1 cup stock made with celery water
½ cup white wine

Wash celery, remove leaves, dice celery into finger-length pieces and boil in salted water for 5 minutes. (Reserve water.)

Meanwhile sauté the bacon and onion in the oil till the onion is golden. Add the rest of the ingredients, including the celery, cover and cook till the celery is tender and the liquid has thickened slightly.

Peperonata
Stewed Peppers

2lb 3oz/1kg various-coloured bell peppers, seeds and pith removed, and sliced into strips
1lb 2oz/½kg fresh or canned tomatoes, peeled and chopped
1 clove garlic, finely chopped
2 onions, finely chopped
1 bayleaf
3 basil leaves
1 heaped tblspn chopped parsley
1 pinch sugar
4fl oz/125ml olive oil
seasoning to taste

Sauté the onions and garlic in the oil till golden and add the peppers and tomatoes. Season and add the bayleaf, basil, parsley and pinch of sugar and gently simmer, half covered, over a medium heat till vegetables are tender.

Serve with roasts or boiled meats, or use as a sauce for pasta.

Spinassi ai Pinoli
Spinach with Pinenuts

This recipe dates back to the Renaissance.

2lb 3oz/1kg spinach
1oz/30g pinenuts
1oz/30g sultanas or raisins soaked in tepid water
2oz/50g butter
salt to taste

Clean and wash the spinach well. Chop and place in a casserole and add salt. Cover with lid. Gently simmer the spinach without adding any water. When tender and cooked, drain and press any excess liquid out with the back of a spoon.

Replace on the heat and heat once more to remove and dry even more for a few minutes.

Melt the butter in a small pan and add the pinenuts and squeezed out sultanas or raisins. Place the spinach on a serving dish and pour over the heated butter, pinenuts and sultanas. Serve hot, and well mixed together.

The pinenuts may be slightly roasted before using.

Segolete Garbo Dolce
Sweet and Sour Pearl Onions

1lb 2oz/½kg small pearl onions (the kind used for pickles)
2 tblspns oil or butter
1 clove
1 bayleaf
½ tspn salt
½ tspn pepper
1½ tspns sugar
½ cup vinegar
½ cup stock
½ tspn flour (if necessary)

Peel onions and place in pot of ice cold water and bring to boil. Boil for 5 minutes. Drain.

Melt butter or oil and add the onions, clove, salt, sugar, bayleaf and stock and cook briskly over a high heat for 5 minutes. Reduce and simmer for 30 minutes or till onions are tender and the sauce is similar to a syrup. Still over the heat, add the vinegar and allow it to evaporate.

If sauce is too liquid mix the flour with a bit of water and stir into the sauce. Add more sugar if desired.

Segolete in Umido
Stewed Pearl Onions

1lb 2oz/½kg pearl (or slightly larger) onions
4 tblspns oil
1 tblspn sugar

Peel onions and boil for 5 minutes in salted water. Drain.

Heat oil and add sugar and cook gently till all becomes brown. Add the onions and gently

Campo Santa Margherita

cook, half covered, till completely tender. Add a little water from time to time if necessary.

Serve with roasts.

Tegoline in Tecia
Pan-cooked String Beans

1lb 2oz/½kg string beans, fresh or frozen
1 tblspn butter
1 tblspn oil
1 onion, chopped
1 small tin peeled tomatoes
seasoning
2 cloves garlic, chopped
2 tblspns chopped parsley
1½ cups stock

Clean and prepare the beans removing the 'string' if using fresh beans.

Heat butter and oil and add onion, parsley and garlic and sauté till tender. Add the rest of the ingredients and simmer, covered, till the beans are tender.

If there is too much liquid left, remove the cover and cook till the liquid is reduced. If, on the other hand, it starts to stick, add a little water.

Verze Sofegae
Suffocated Cabbage

Once again, don't be alarmed – it's really only braised cabbage!

1 small head cabbage
3 tblspns oil
2 cloves garlic
1 tspn minced rosemary leaves
1 tblspn tomato sauce (*see* Sauces) or equivalent

Wash and slice the cabbage into thin strips.

Heat oil and add all the ingredients except the tomato and simmer over low heat, covered, until cabbage is tender. When tender, add the tomato and cook a further 5 minutes.

Verze in Tecia
Pan-cooked Cabbage

1 small head cabbage
1 large onion, chopped
4 tblspns oil
seasoning to taste

Wash and thinly slice the cabbage. Heat the oil and add the onion and cabbage and cook over low heat till both are tender and slightly golden. Season to taste.

Torta de Verdure
Vegetable Pie

This is a dish which dates back to fifteenth-century Venice. A similar recipe is found in a fourteenth-century book by someone called Platino. In the fourteenth-century it was cooked on top of the coals with a copper lid placed on top of the pie and more coals placed on top of the copper lid. It's usually made up of leftovers.

½lb/225g shortcrust pastry (made with 8oz/225g flour,
4oz/125g butter or fat, a pinch sugar, a pinch
cinnamon and a pinch cloves
and about 2 tblspns cold water)
14oz/400g spinach, beetgreens or any other green
vegetable, cooked, and in the case of spinach and
beetgreens, thoroughly drained of juices
5oz/150g leftover meat
cheese (optional)
1 egg to bind (optional)

Keep pastry in fridge till needed, then roll out half and line a pie dish about 8in/20cm in diameter.

Sauté the vegetables in a little butter or with a little bacon. Mix this together with chopped meat and optional cheese and bind if desired with beaten egg. (This is not one hundred per cent necessary.) Roll out lid for top of pie and seal edges by pressing well together and fluting the edges.

Bake pie in oven at 400°F/200°C for 20 minutes or until golden.

7 SALSE

SAUCES

"Duck Hunting in the Lagoon" (after Pietro Longhi)

Peverada
Peppered or Piquant Sauce

There is no translation for 'peverada' or 'pearà' (*see* recipe below) and they are usually referred to by their original name. This sauce is served with roast chicken, pigeon or game birds. If using game birds then use their livers added to the sauce instead of the full amount of chicken livers.

3½oz/100g chicken livers
2 anchovy fillets
1 large piece of lemon peel
1 tblspn chopped parsley
2 cloves garlic
5 tblspns olive oil
lemon juice
vinegar or dry white wine
2 tblspns breadcrumbs

Finely chop or mince the livers, the anchovies, lemon peel, parsley and 1 clove garlic. Mix well together and add the breadcrumbs.

In a pan heat the oil and sauté the other garlic clove and when golden remove and discard. Add the liver mixture and season well. Gently cook and add a little lemon juice for added flavour and a dash of vinegar or wine. Mix well and after a few minutes serve.

Variation 1
Add 1 tblspn Parmesan cheese to the liver mixture.

Variation 2
Add a good pinch of ginger. This variation has a touch of the East!

Variation 3
Add some pickled onions or chillies and some capers, and dilute the final sauce with the juices from the roast.

Variation 4
Add 1 small kidney, skinned and very finely chopped, and braised with some parsley, sage and minced rosemary leaves. For another touch of the East, a grating of orange rind and a little candied peel may be added.

Variation 5
This stems from the Middle Ages. Instead of using just lemon juice, use half lemon and half pomegranate juice.

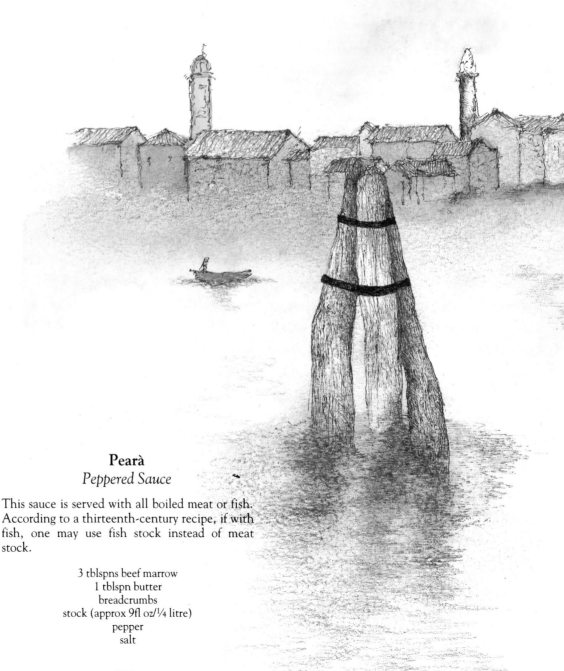

Pearà
Peppered Sauce

This sauce is served with all boiled meat or fish. According to a thirteenth-century recipe, if with fish, one may use fish stock instead of meat stock.

3 tblspns beef marrow
1 tblspn butter
breadcrumbs
stock (approx 9fl oz/¼ litre)
pepper
salt

The Lagoon - San Michele and Murano

Sally Spector 1987

In an earthenware, heatproof dish, melt the butter and add the marrow and melt this too. Add enough breadcrumbs to absorb all the fat and as soon as this is done add a little stock and a generous amount of pepper. Add salt to taste. Gently simmer over a very low heat, stirring from time to time, for at least 2 hours.

Sugo de Pomodori
Tomato Sauce

This may be used for all types of pasta, gnocchi *raviolini* and so on, as well as for gravies and other dishes instead of plain tomatoes. For a quicker sauce, omit the carrot and celery.

1lb 2oz/500g unskinned jam tomatoes (long type)
or 14oz/400g tinned, peeled tomatoes
1 clove garlic
1 small onion
1 small carrot
1 stalk celery
3 tblspns parsley
2 tblspns basil
¾oz/20g butter
1 tspn sugar
2 tblspns olive oil
salt and freshly ground pepper

In a copper or earthenware pot melt the butter and oil and add the celery, carrot, onion and parsley finely chopped together. Cover the pot and cook over a moderate heat for a few minutes, stirring from time to time.

Add the tomatoes, cut into large pieces, the basil and the garlic and recover the pot and allow to cook over a low heat for 15 minutes. Add the salt, sugar and pepper and mouli, blend or sieve the sauce.

Return to a low heat and gently simmer for another 25 minutes until the water from the tomatoes has been consumed and the sauce has thickened. Do not overcook as it will tend to become acid in taste.

This sauce may be bottled and sealed like jam to be used when needed.

Salsa de Anara
Duck Sauce

This is used for *bigoli*, the type of spahetti made with wholewheat flour, typical of the area.

gizzard, liver, heart etc of duck
1½oz/40g butter
2 tblspns olive oil
3 sage leaves
1 tblspn white wine
seasoning

Finely mince the gizzard, heart etc separately from the liver. Mince the liver. Heat the oil and the butter in a pan and gently sauté the minced gizzard, heart etc and sage, till they become nicely browned. Add the wine and cook for about 10 minutes. Add the minced liver and mix well. Season and serve on *bigoli* or spaghetti.

Haroseth
Haroseth

This is a Jewish recipe for a type of sauce or marmalade, served at Pesach (Passover) or Easter with roast lamb. The recipe goes back to the 1200s.

3 apples, peeled and sliced
2 pears, peeled and sliced
1 glass sweet white wine
2oz/50g pinenuts
2oz/50g almonds slivers
7oz/200g pitted dates, sliced
3½oz/100g raisins
3½oz/100g prunes, sliced
3½oz/100g sugar *or* 5oz/150g honey
pinch cinnamon

optional:
1 tblspn candied peel
1 tblspn walnuts
1 tblspn pistachio nuts
1 tblspn finely chopped dried figs
juice of 1 lemon or orange
pinch ginger
pinch nutmeg
pinch cloves

Put all ingredients into a pot and gently simmer. Add any or all of optional ingredients. To thicken sauce slightly, use a little cornflour.

Entrance to the Ghetto

Mostarda Fina alla Venessiana
Venetian Sweet and Sharp Sauce

This recipe differs from those of other regions, like Cremona, because all the other areas usually have large chunks of fruit left in the sauce (so that it is then really a type of jam or jelly). The sweet and sour mixture shows a Renaissance influence.

2lb 3oz/1kg quinces, peeled
2lb 3oz/1kg pears, peeled
2lb 3oz/1kg apples, peeled
sugar equal to total weight of cooked quinces, pears and apples
1lb 2oz/500g candied fruit peel (limes and oranges)
1 tblspn or to taste mustard (preferably French, granular type)
white wine must (made by boiling 26fl oz/750ml wine with 9fl oz/250ml honey till liquid reduces to a third)

Depip the fruit and cook each individually till tender in wine must. Sieve each individually. The puréed fruit should result quite firm. Add the weight of the cooked fruit in sugar (a little less if so desired). Add the candied fruit, diced small, and the mustard to taste. (Mustard powder may also be used instead of the granular type).
Conserve in jars with a lid and sterilized if possible. Serve with meats, preferably boiled, or with cold cuts.

Salsa de Pomo Granato
Pomegranate Sauce

This is used with sweetbreads or game birds and dates back to the early 1600s. In Bartolomeo Stefani's book of this period, *L'arte di ben cucinare* (The art of good cooking), he refers to a Venetian chef, Guilio Cesare Tirelli, who, he says, is most superior and taught Stefani all his recipes.
Ambergris is a wax-like substance found floating in the Malayan, Madagascar and Japanese Seas and inside spermwhales, and is formed by the decomposition of cuttlefish. It was much used in the Middle Ages and is still appreciated in Eastern dishes today. It is also used in the perfume industry. However, spermwhales are becoming increasingly rare because of being hunted and there are now international whaling agreements to protect them.

18fl oz/500ml pomegranate juice (if using fresh pomegranates and not tinned, use a juice extractor)
6oz/180g sugar
1 grain ambergris or a little rosewater

Simmer all the ingredients together without a lid over a low heat till reduced by half.

Salsa Verde
Green Sauce

Serve with fish or boiled meat. During the Renaissance, instead of lemon juice *agresto* (the juice of unripe, sour grapes) or pomegranate juice was used.

1 hardboiled egg
1 anchovy fillet
juice ½ lemon
4fl oz/125ml olive oil
1 slice bread, soaked in chicken stock and squeezed to remove excess
1 clove garlic

optional:
3 tblspns pinenuts
2 tblspns capers
1 chilli pepper
cayenne pepper to taste

Blend together all the ingredients till they make a fine sauce.

8 DOLSI

PUDDINGS, CAKES, BISCUITS AND SWEETS

Crema Frita
Fried Cream

This can be bought in most fresh pasta shops and in some bakeries. It is even more delicious freshly made at home and eaten while still tepid.

3oz/90g white flour
2½oz/75g sugar
2 eggs
18fl oz/½ litre milk
grated rind of 1 small lemon
oil or margarine for frying
flour or breadcrumbs
sugar for dusting

Put the sugar and flour into a pot, and add the milk, over a low heat, stirring continuously. The stirring should be done in the shape of a figure of eight in order to pass always through the centre of the pot thus preventing the mixture from catching. Cook for 5 minutes.

Remove from the heat and add the eggs one at a time and the grated lemon peel.

Return to the heat and continue stirring for another 5 minutes. Wet a large dish and pour the cream into this so that it is about 1¼in/3cm high and leave to cool.

Cut diagonally so that each piece is diamond shaped. Dust in the flour or breadcrumbs and fry in the hot oil or margarine, on both sides.

Sprinkle with sugar and serve.

Pan de Spagna
Italian Sponge Cake

This recipe literally translated means Spanish bread. This is a *never-fail* sponge cake that has yet to be beaten. I discovered this one day when I was all out of butter but in the mood to bake a cake.

5 eggs, yolks and whites separated
1½ cups sugar
1¼ cups white cake flour, sifted
1 tspn vanilla essence
½ tspn grated lemon rind

Put the egg yolks and sugar in a mixing bowl and beat till lemon coloured. Add the sifted flour, a little at a time, mixing in well. Add the essence and rind.

Beat the egg whites until stiff but not dry and fold into the flour mixture.

Butter and flour a cake tin about 10in/25cm in diameter. Pour in the cake mix and bake in a moderate oven for 40 minutes.

Turn out on to a cake rack and cool.

Tirame-Sú 1
Pick-Me-Up Cake 1

This is a 'new' recipe, only found in the Venice area. This version is the one served in restaurants.

1 Italian Sponge Cake (*see above*) baked in a
14in/35cm cake tin
½ cup strong black coffee
3½fl oz/100ml kirsch or Tia Maria or any other
favourite liqueur
1lb 2oz/500g cream cheese sweetened with icing sugar
to taste
unsweetened cocoa powder

Cool the sponge cake and split in half. Mix together the liqueur and coffee and carefully sprinkle half over bottom half of cake. Spread some cream cheese over this half and place the second half on top of this. Sprinkle the top of the cake with the rest of the liqueur and coffee and spread the rest of the cream cheese over the top and sides of the cake. Sieve a thickish layer of unsweetened cocoa powder over the top and

Sally Spector 1987

Corte de la Raffineria

transfer to a serving plate. This cake should only be about 2in/5cm in height and should be fairly moist without crumbling inside.

Tirame-Sú 2
Pick-Me-Up Cake 2

This is the version made at home.

6 egg yolks
3½fl oz/100ml Marsala
3½fl oz/100ml dry white wine
3oz/80g icing sugar (or more to taste)
1lb 2oz/500g marscarpone or cream cheese
24 Savoy biscuits ('ladies' fingers')
3½fl oz/100ml Marsala
½ cup strong black coffee
unsweetened cocoa powder

Mix the first 5 ingredients together to make a cream, but if making this for children or teetotallers leave out Marsala and white wine. Dip the biscuits in the Marsala and coffee mixed (once again leave out Marsala if so desired) but take care not to make biscuits so soggy that they break. Line a dish about 10in/25cm square with a layer of biscuits and a layer of the cream. Repeat, till all the ingredients have been used, ending with a cream layer. Sprinkle a thin layer of unsweetened cocoa powder on top and place dish in refrigerator for a few hours.

Fugazza Pasquale
Easter Cake

As its name implies, this is usually made only around Easter.

9fl oz/250ml milk
½oz/15g brewer's yeast (fresh)
3 egg yolks
4oz/125g sugar
3½oz/100g butter or margarine, at room temperature
14oz/400g white cake flour
1 tspn grated lemon rind
pinch salt
3 tblspns minced, peeled almonds

Heat the milk till just tepid and dissolve the yeast in this. Pour into a large mixing bowl and add the sugar and salt, and then the eggs and butter alternating with the flour. Mix and knead well and cover with damp cloth and leave to rise overnight in a warm place.

The next morning knead once again and add the lemon peel.

Butter and flour a 10in/25cm diameter cake tin (one which is deep) and place the dough in this and allow to rise once more for a few hours in a warm place.

Brush dough with some milk and sprinkle the chopped almonds on top. Bake in a hot oven (425°F/220°C) for 45 minutes.

Fritele
Venetian Doughnut

These are eaten at Carnival and every *pasticeria* and bar sells them during this period. This is a traditional recipe using yeast. The doughnuts become hard after twenty-four hours and therefore must be eaten the same day.

1lb 2oz/500g white cake flour
1oz/30g brewer's yeast, dissolved in a little tepid milk
2½oz/75g sugar
pinch salt
½ glass white wine or milk
1 handful raisins, soaked in the wine or milk
grated rind of 1 lemon
35fl oz/1 litre oil for frying
2 tblspns pinenuts
icing sugar for dusting
2 tblspns candied peel (optional)

Mix all the ingredients together and knead well. Leave to rise in a warm place till double in bulk (about 1 hour).

Heat the oil till hot and drop tablespoonfuls of mixture into hot oil till golden-brown all over and cooked through.

Dust with icing sugar.

Fritele de Ilona
Ilona's Doughnuts

These are not strictly traditional because they are made with baking powder, but more and more people are using it these days and it does tend to make them stay soft longer. Canadian applies are used because they are softer and disintegrate without leaving wet pieces in the doughnuts.

1lb 2oz/500g white flour
2 Canadian apples, grated
2½oz/75g butter, melted
3–4 tblspns sugar
3 eggs
3½oz/100g raisins, plumped in tepid water
½oz/15g baking powder
grated peel of 1 orange and its juice
1 liqueur glass Marsala
or ½ liqueur glass grappa
35fl oz/1 litre oil for frying
icing sugar for dusting

Sift the flour a little at a time into the beaten eggs, beating in at each stage till all the flour is used. Add the sugar and the salt to the mixture. Add the rest of the ingredients and mix well. If too thick add a little milk.

Drop tablespoonfuls into hot oil and remove when golden-brown all over and cooked in the centre.

Dust with icing sugar.

Galani o Crostoli Venessiani
Venetian Biscuits

These are traditional Carnival fare like *Fritele* (*see* above). No doubt they are another inheritance from the East (via Marco Polo?) as they are a type of flaky pastry much like Chinese pastries. However they are served with icing sugar instead of a treacle-like syrup and they are cut into different shapes.

5oz/150g flour
1 egg
2 eggshell halves of wine (white)
1 tspn sugar
pinch salt
soft butter (as much as needed)
icing sugar for dusting

These are small quantities but it is advisable to repeat the process rather than to double or treble up.

Mix all these ingredients together except the butter and knead well so that you have a fine pliable dough.

When this is done divide into three equal parts like three flat meatballs. Take some of the soft butter and spread it gently over the top of the first piece and not quite to the edges. Place the second piece of dough on top of this and repeat, then place the third piece of dough on the second but do not butter.

Now with a rolling pin, roll out the three layers together on a floured table or surface into one very thin layer as thinly as you can. Then, if you have someone to help you, gently pull the dough on each side so that it becomes transparent and even thinner.

Replace the dough on the floured table or surface and with a pasta wheel or knife cut out long strips about ¾in/2cm wide and then cut these strips into pieces about 2–2¼in/5–6cm long – these can be twisted into bows.

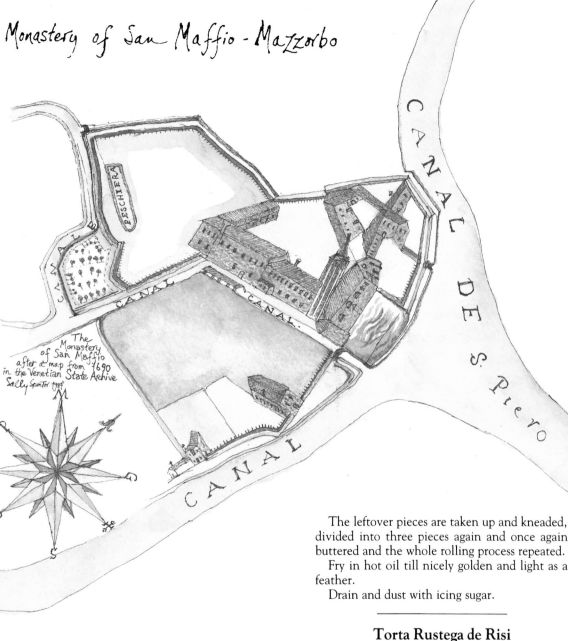

Monastery of San Maffio - Mazzorbo

PESCHIERA

CANAL

THE CANAL

CANAL DE S. Piero

CANAL

The Monastery of San Maffio after a map from 1690 in the Venetian State Archive
Sally Spector 1994

6oz/175g rice
9fl oz/¼ litre milk
3½oz/100g sugar
2oz/50g butter
grated rind of 1 lemon
grated rind of 1 orange
2 eggs
2 tblspns sugar
3½oz/100g minced, peeled almonds

Put rice in cold salted water. Bring to the boil and boil for 5 minutes. Drain well and allow to cool.

Heat the milk and as it starts to rise add 9fl oz/¼ litre hot water, the 3½oz/100g sugar, butter, cold rice and lemon and orange rind. Leave to simmer uncovered for 15 minutes.

Meanwhile in a bowl beat the 2 egg yolks together with the 2 tblspns sugar and then add the 2 egg whites which have been beaten till stiff and the minced almonds. Add a tblspn of the rice mixture which has finished cooking and mix this together. Add to the rice mixture in the pot.

Butter and breadcumb a cake pan about 10in/25cm in diameter. Add mixture. Bake in a hot oven for ½ hour.

This is eaten cold.

Zaletti
Yellow Biscuits

10½oz/300g yellow flour (finely ground yellow maizemeal)
1 tblspn white flour
2 egg yolks
5oz/150g butter, melted
5oz/150g sugar
3½oz/100g raisins, soaked in warm water
3½oz/100g pinenuts

Mix all the ingredients very well with a wooden spoon, form into finger-length rolls and place on a greased baking tray and bake in a hot oven for ½ hour.

These are eaten with a sweet wine.

The leftover pieces are taken up and kneaded, divided into three pieces again and once again buttered and the whole rolling process repeated.

Fry in hot oil till nicely golden and light as a feather.

Drain and dust with icing sugar.

Torta Rustega de Risi
Rustic Rice Cake

This is an old recipe traditionally made for Redentore (*see* Traditional Feast Days). It is taken and eaten the night before while watching the fireworks display from the decorated boats.

Ice Cream Vendor - Campo Santa Maddelena

GELATI

Sally Spector
1982

Baicoli

These are well known Venetian biscuits sold throughout the world. They are rather time consuming to make but well worth it! They could be described as a wafer-type rusk.

13oz/370g flour
½oz/15g brewer's yeast melted in a little tepid water
2oz/50g butter
pinch salt
2oz/50g butter, melted
1 egg white, beaten
milk

Take 2½oz/70g of the flour and mix together with the yeast to form a dough. Knead well and cut a cross on the top with a sharp knife. Cover with a clean cloth (preferably muslin) and leave to rise in a warm place.

When it has doubled in bulk, add the rest of the flour, the butter, salt and egg white. Knead very well, moistening occasionally with a little tepid milk so that a fine pliable dough is formed.

Divide the dough into 4 pieces and roll out into shapes of sausage thickness (about 1¼in/3cm) and 12in/30cm long. Place on a buttered baking tray a good distance apart and cover with a muslin cloth. Leave for 1½ hours to rise and then bake in preheated hot oven for 10 minutes till the shapes take on a pinkish colour.

Remove and cover once again with muslin cloth and leave for 48 hours. Then slice the rolls as one would a salami – ie at a slight angle and thinly.

Bake these biscuits in a moderate oven till golden on both sides and quite dried out. Leave to cool.

Serve with *zabaione* (*see* below).

Zabaione
Whipped Marsala Custard

per person:
2 egg yolks
2 tspns sugar or to taste
1 small glass Marsala or sweet sherry

Put the egg yolks, sugar and Marsala in a large bowl over a pan of simmering water, or in a large double boiler.

Whisk with a hand or electric beater over the hot water till the mixture becomes pale and fluffy and leaves a trail in the bowl as you lift the beater away. Do not boil or overheat as this custard will curdle.

As soon as it is ready pour into warmed glasses and serve with above biscuits or macaroons.

Pinza

This is one of the most antique traditional cake recipes. It is a 'rustic' cake.

1lb 2oz/½kg yellow flour (finely ground yellow maizemeal)
3½oz/100g white cake flour
2 eggs
7oz/200g raisins
7oz/200g dried figs, cut into small pieces
1oz/30g baking powder
2oz/50g fennel seeds
2oz/50g lard
enough milk to make a fairly soft mixture (the yellow flour absorbs a lot of liquid while cooking)

Mix all the ingredients to form a rather soft mixture and place in a greased rectangular or round cake tin. (In the shops it is made into a large rectangle in order to cut it into squares and sell per square.)

Bake in a moderate oven. Test by piercing with a toothpick. If the toothpick comes out clean it is done. (It is difficult to say how long this will take, because if the weather is humid, maizemeal absorbs more liquid.)

Perseghi (o Pere) Ripieni
Stuffed Peaches or Pears

In the North of England they say 'Apple pie without cheese is like a kiss without a squeeze': in Venice they say 'Al contadino no fa sapere quanto e buono il formaggio con le pere' ('Never let on to the countryman or farmer how good cheese is with pears').

4 fresh peaches or pears
or 8 canned halves
2½ tblspns lemon juice
2oz/50g Gorgonzola
1oz/25g soft butter
2 tblspns crushed walnuts
sour cream to cover each filling

Peel and stone fresh fruit or dry the canned ones. Mix together all ingredients except the sour cream and fill fruit halves. Chill these and just before serving pour some sour cream over each half.

Pasta Frolla 1
Shortcrust Pastry 1

8 heaped tblspns flour
8 level tblspns butter
pinch salt
1 heaped tblspn sugar (if using for sweet dishes)
2 tblspns ice-cold water

Place bowl in refrigerator before using. Cut the butter into the flour in bowl and 'rub in' till it resembles breadcrumbs. Add the water – enough so that the dough just comes away from the sides of the bowl. Cover and place in refrigerator for at least 15 minutes before rolling out.

Pasta Frolla 2
Mildred's Shortcrust Pastry

1lb 2oz/½kg white self-raising flour
12oz/350g butter and fat
ice-cold water to bind
pinch salt
1 tblspn sugar (if using for sweet dishes)

In a cold bowl, as above, cut the butter and fat into the flour till the pieces are the size of a walnut. Don't rub the fat in. Add the water, till pastry comes away from bowl. Remove from bowl and pat into a rectangle and fold into three as for puff pastry. Cover and place in refrigerator for at least 15 minutes.

Bussolai a la Venessiana
Ring-shaped Crisp Biscuits

2lb 3oz/1kg white flour
3 eggs
11oz/300g sugar
7oz/200g butter, melted
grated rind of 1 lemon
pinch cinnamon
½ glass sweet white wine

Knead all the ingredients well, till they form a pliable dough. Roll out into finger-thick, sausage-like rolls 10in/25cm in length. Join the two ends together, brush shapes with melted butter and place on greased baking tray.

Bake in moderate oven till nicely golden.

Torta de Gnente
Simple or Made-of-nothing Cake

1lb 2oz/500g white cake flour, sifted
butter (enough to make a smooth paste or dough)
3½oz/100g icing sugar
pinch salt

Put the flour in a bowl and mix in enough butter to make a smooth dough. Add the icing sugar and pinch of salt and place in a round, greased, preferably copper, cake tin.

Bake in moderate oven till cooked through

(about ½ hour). This cooks even better if the heat is from below and above.

Perseghi in Giazzo
Iced Peaches

4 fresh, not too ripe peaches
8 almond halves, skinned
or 8 small macaroons
1 liqueur glass anisette or any other liqueur
sugar for sprinkling

Parboil the peaches for 2–3 minutes. Remove, drain, cut in half and remove stone. Place an almond half or macaroon in each peach half and sprinkle peach half with sugar. Place halves on a large plate and sprinkle with the liqueur.

Cover with a plate and leave in the fridge for 3 hours.

Crocantini
Toffee-covered Nuts and Fruit

9oz/250g icing sugar
1 tblspn glucose
1 tblspn water
3 tblspns mixed whole nuts
(walnuts, almonds and hazelnuts)
some grapes
some fresh cherries, stones removed
about 4 prunes
about 4 dates
about 4 fresh apricots, halved

Wash and dry well the various types of fruit and nuts. In a pot place the sugar, water and glucose and heat over medium to high heat and stir till the sugar has melted and becomes a golden colour or hard crack. Pierce each piece of fruit and nut with a toothpick and dip into the toffee. Then place separately on sheet of greaseproof paper till hardened.

Note: these are still sold in the streets and about four fruit or nuts or a mixture are put on to very thin wire skewers, dipped into the toffee, allowed to hardened and then twisted into greaseproof paper.

Chifel
Apricot- or Almond-filled Croissants

These are an inheritance from the Austrian occupation and are eaten, as in Austria, for breakfast.

12oz/350g flour
large pinch salt
2oz/50g castor sugar
9fl oz/250ml lukewarm milk
9oz/250g butter
1 egg, beaten
some extra beaten egg for brushing
soft water icing
ground almonds (optional)

filling 1:
apricot jam

filling 2:
2oz/50g ground almonds
2oz/50g castor sugar
little beaten egg

Sift the flour with the salt into a large bowl, cream the yeast with the sugar until liquid and add to the lukewarm milk, add 2oz/50g of the butter and mix till dissolved, and then add the beaten egg. Pour this then into the flour and mix to a smooth dough. Cover the dough and leave at room temperature for about an hour or till it has doubled in size.

Punch down the dough and turn on to a lightly floured board or table. Knead lightly. Roll out to an oblong and cover two-thirds of the dough with half the remaining butter, divided into walnut-size pieces. Fold unbuttered section towards buttered section and then fold again till in three.

Roll out again and repeat once again with the rest of the butter. Roll and fold twice more and leave again for 15 minutes. Chill the dough for a short time.

If using filling 2, mix almonds and sugar together to form a paste and bind with a little egg. The paste must be firm.

Roll out chilled dough to about ½in/1cm thick and cut into a triangle measuring 4in/10cm between two points and 6½in/17cm down to the last point. Place a little filling between the two points 4in/10cm apart, but not too near the

Church of San Martino

edge. Roll up towards last point so that it looks like a croissant. Gently bend into half moon and allow to prove.

Brush with a little egg and bake at 350–400°F/ 180–200°C for 25 minutes or until golden-brown.

Brush while still warm with water icing and sprinkle with a little ground almonds if desired.

Krapfen
Austrian Doughnut filled with Apricot Jam

7oz/200g white flour
2oz/50g butter (at room temperature)
½oz/15g fresh yeast
1 whole egg
1 egg yolk
2oz/50g icing sugar
2oz/50g castor sugar
oil for deep frying
apricot jam for filling

Dissolve the yeast with a little lukewarm water and pour mixture into a bowl with 2oz/50g of the flour. Keep adding a little water (lukewarm) till a soft ball has formed. Cover and leave in a warm place for about 25 minutes until double in bulk.

Sift the remaining flour into a bowl with the icing sugar. Make a well in the middle and add the whole egg, the egg yolk and the butter cut up into small pieces.

Work all this together, adding the risen yeast ball till the dough does not stick to the sides of the bowl. Flour this ball of dough slightly and cover and leave to rise in a warm place till double in size (about 2 hours).

Punch down dough and knead slightly and roll out to ¼in/½cm thick. Cut into round disks 3¼in/8cm in diameter.

Place a little jam on the centre of a disk and lightly dampen the disk's edges; place on top of this another disk and lightly press the two edges together. Leave these to rise for 15 minutes.

Heat the oil till hot and fry rounds for about 2 minutes on each side till golden-brown.

Remove, drain and dust with castor sugar.

Orecchie di Ammon
Hammon's Ears

Hammon, Lot's son, wanted to destroy the Jewish race. Great delight accompanies the crunching of these 'ears'. The recipe was brought to Venice in the twelfth century.

flour (as much as needed)
3 eggs
4 tblspns oil
3 tblspns sugar
pinch salt
egg white for brushing
oil for frying
honey or syrup or icing sugar

Mix the first five ingredients together to form a soft pliable dough. Roll out thinly as for the *crostoli* or *galani* (*see* above). Cut into strips about 1in/2½cm wide and 6in/15cm long. Brush a little egg white on the tip of one end and join the two ends together to form an 'ear'. Fry in hot oil till golden (as for the *crostoli* or *galani*).

Remove and drain and dust with icing sugar. Some families brush them with honey or syrup.

Mandolato
Almond Toffee or Nougat

This recipe is supposed to have been invented in 1852 by a Venetian pharmacist called Marani who made it famous all over the world. Actually it goes back as far as the Renaissance.

11oz/300g honey
3 egg whites, beaten till stiff
pinch cinnamon

1lb 2oz/500g peeled almonds
11oz/300g sugar and 4oz/100g water boiled
to hard crack stage
5oz/150g hazelnuts, skinned
5oz/150g candied peel

(if only almonds are desired
increase them to 1½lb/700g)

Heat the honey over a very low heat over a bain-marie, stirring for about ½ hour till it reaches hard crack stage.

Cool and then carefully stir in the beaten eggs and stir over heat for another 5 minutes. It will rise and become foamy.

Add sugar and beat mixture till it starts hardening. Add the pinch of cinnamon and the almonds, nuts and peel and pour into a flat baking tray (about 10in/25cm square) lined with rice paper or sheets of wafer. Put another layer of rice paper on top. Weigh down and leave to cool.

Cut into desired lengths or pieces.

Tortion
Venetian Apple Strudel

This is another inheritance from Austria.

14oz/400g white cake flour
4 tblspns oil
or 4oz/100g butter
2oz/50g sugar
2 eggs

apple filling:
2lb 3oz/1kg apples
4 tblspns sugar
3–4 tblspns sultanas
3½oz/100g pinenuts
2½oz/75g candied peel
2oz/50g skinned almonds
2oz/50g skinned walnuts
2½oz/75g butter, diced
pinch of cinnamon

icing sugar for sprinkling
beaten egg for brushing
butter for brushing

Sieve the flour, make a well in the centre and add the oil or butter, the sugar, and the eggs. Knead these all together well adding a little tepid water a little at a time in order to obtain a light, soft and smooth dough. Beat it against a large rolling board many times so that it becomes elastic. Form into a ball and cover with a cloth and leave to rest for at least an hour.

In the meantime peel and slice the apples and leave to soak in lemon water, then dry. Mince or finely chop the nuts. Soak the sultanas in tepid water for 10 minutes then drain well.

Roll out dough lightly into a large rectangle

and evenly spread all the filling ingredients down the middle (the apple pieces should be quite dry), sprinkle with the sugar, cinnamon and diced butter and roll up. Place on greased baking sheet join side down and bend into half-moon shape. Brush with some egg and butter and bake in a hot oven (425°F/220°C) for 15 minutes then decrease heat to 375–400°F/190–200°C and bake for a further 45 minutes.

Leave to cool and sprinkle with icing sugar.

Favette o 'Fave dei Morti'
Bean-size Nutty Biscuits or 'Beans for All Souls'

These biscuits are traditionally eaten around All Saints' and All Souls' Days (1 and 2 November).

11oz/300g icing sugar
2 egg whites
juice of 1 lemon
6oz/175g pinenuts, finely minced
1 tspn cocoa powder
few drops cochineal
some white cake flour for dusting

version 2:
4oz/125g flour
pinch cinnamon

Palazzo da Mula – Murano

Beat the sugar and egg whites (and flour and cinnamon for version 2) in a large bowl for about ½ hour, adding a drop of lemon juice at a time. Remove 4 tblspns of the mixture and put aside.

Add the pinenuts and mix well together. Place on rolling board and roll out into a sausage shape.

Add the 4 tblspns put aside on top of this and roll together. Divide into 3 parts.

One is kept white, to the second add the cocoa and to the third add the cochineal.

When these have been well blended, form into small balls slightly bigger than a hazelnut. Place on greased and floured baking sheet and bake in a moderate oven till done but not browned (about 15–20 minutes).

Storti
Rolled Biscuits

These biscuits are made in the same way as ginger snaps and are famous in Venice. They are eaten with fresh cream whipped up with a little sugar and an optional drop of liqueur. The cream and biscuits together are known as 'Panna coi Storti'.

11oz/300g sugar
11oz/300g white cake flour
1oz/30g butter
pinch salt
4fl oz/125ml milk and cream

Mix all ingredients together till fairly liquid. Drop teaspoonsful on a greased baking sheet and bake in a moderate oven for about 10 minutes. Remove from oven and roll around a greased wooden spoon. Serve with fresh cream as described above.

Note: if you are fortunate to be in the possession of a wafer iron (the two-handled affair which is used to make wafers for communion), you can drop some of the batter in this and then roll when done.

An easy way to roll these – or ginger snaps – I discovered one frustrating day is to cut 2in/5cm squares of greaseproof paper, place these on the baking tray and drop mixture on to them. When the biscuits are done lift up the paper and

*Piazza San Marco
– seen from Caffè Florian*

Sally Spector 1983

mixture together and roll around a greased spoon handle (paper outwards). The paper comes away cleanly and a neat snap or *storto* is left on the handle to slide off without breakages.

Persegada o Cotognata
Quince Preserve

St Martin on his horse in quince preserve is traditional on his feast day (11 November). Also traditional in Venice is St Martin made in Venetian biscuit or sweet shortcrust pastry, decorated with water icing and royal icing in various colours and with silver balls and hundreds and thousands sprinkled over.

2lb 3oz/1kg quinces
1¾lb/800g (approx) sugar

Cook the quinces in a large pot of boiling water for 4–5 minutes. Take off heat, skin fruit, reserving pulp and weigh pulp. Weigh the same weight in sugar and cook together till well thickened (about 10 minutes).

Place in moulds like that of St Martin on his horse or any fancy small tart or *petit four* moulds, having first sugared the moulds well. Leave jelly in moulds till cold, preferably for 24 hours.

If using St Martin moulds, after taking out the jelly decorate it with various-sized confectioner's silver balls.

Rosada alla Veneziana
Baked Custard

This is a recipe from 1819.

6 eggs
5oz/150g sugar
35fl oz/1 litre milk
1 tspn rosewater, orange-blossom water
or cinnamon water
sugar for sprinkling

Mix all the ingredients together well and strain twice. Butter a baking dish well, and pour mixture into the dish. This may then be baked as it is or in a larger dish with water (like a bain-marie), in a cool oven for about 30 minutes.

When set sprinkle with sugar and place under grill to caramelize.

Calicioni
Almond Biscuits

A recipe from the 1500s.

1lb 2oz/½kg shortcrust pastry 1 (*see* above), made with cold rosewater rather than plain water
1lb/450g almonds, soaked overnight and then finely ground
1lb/450g sugar (or less to taste)
1 tblspn (approx) rosewater or roseolio (liqueur) to amalgamate almond paste

Mix almonds, sugar and rosewater well together forming a firm paste. Roll out pastry and cut into squares or rounds.

Place a little of the filling on top of one square and cover with another square.

Press edges to seal (so that they now look like ravioli) and bake in oven at 325-350°F/160–180°C, taking care not to burn them as these cook quickly. They should take about 10–15 minutes.

TRADITIONAL FEAST DAYS

Shrovetide

Especially the last Thursday of Carnival (usually the end of March), large quantities of *bigoli* (wholewheat spaghetti), gnocchi (potato dumplings) and *fritele* (deep-fried cakes) are consumed, as well as *crostoli* and *galani* (these are deep-fried, sweet, flakey pastries).

Lent

During Lent fish is usually consumed, as well as frogs, *bacalà* (dried cod), omelettes—made with shrimps, rice and wild asparagus (*bruscandoli*—scientific name *luppola*—as we know it 'hops').

Easter

Lamb is usually eaten and it is one of the few occasions when all butchers carry lamb—strangely Venetians say that summer is too hot to eat lamb!

Ascension Day

Pig's trotter is eaten, plain or stuffed. On this day Venice is officially married to the sea; this dates back to the eleventh century and is an outward sign of her domination of the Adriatic Sea. The Doge would go out (and the mayor still does) on a boat called 'Bucintoro' (a gaily painted, old sea-galley) to the Lido island port, followed by a vast procession of various types of privately owned boats decked out for the occasion. The patriarch would bless the sea with holy water and the Doge, from a little door in the prow, would throw a gold ring into the sea, pronouncing the words 'In sign of eternal domination, we, the Doge of Venice, marry you, oh sea!'.

This symbolic ceremony initiated a series of fairs and events lasting fifteen days and culminating in St Mark's Square with a kind of art and craft show by all the artisans of Venice.

San Marco (St Mark's Day) 25 April

To celebrate Venice's patron saint, the Evangelist St Mark. The tradition is that the Venetian men buy a long stemmed red rosebud for the woman or women close to his heart. This includes sisters, mothers, grandmothers, wives etc...! All around the city and on the nearby islands stands are erected where Red Cross volunteers sell these roses.

Redentore (Redeemer Day) Third Sunday of July

The day of the Redeemer is celebrated by all Venetians in a big way. Anyone who possesses a boat, no matter what size it may be, decks it out with lanterns and leafy boughs and, if it's large enough, places a table in the centre and chairs around it and away they go, with plenty to eat and drink, to enjoy their party in the lagoon till the fireworks display which starts at about 11.30 at night, after which, they all head out through the port mouth at the Lido island to swim and carry on the party.

The next day it is traditional to walk across the pontoon bridge built from Venice across the Grand Canal to the Salute island and then from Salute island across the Guidecca Canal to the Redeemer church on the Guidecca island. This church was built as thanks to the Redeemer for liberating the city from the plague. It was designed by Palladio. Sardines or sole in *saor* (sweet and sour sauce), rice cake and roast duck are traditional fare.

Historical Regatta First Sunday in September

Essentially a regatta for gondoliers and oarsmen and an historical procession of ancient sailing vessels, centuries old, bedecked by women and manned by oarsmen, traditionally dressed in the manner of the period of their particular vessel. From one to nine oarsmen may row one of the many types of boats which compete in this 4½ mile race. This race dates back the 1300s. The Grand Canal from the basin of St Mark's is lined on both sides by people all eager to get a view of this fascinating sight.

In the evening the Venetians go out in their boats as described before for the Redeemer Day, and eat out in their boats. This way of 'eating out' is called *i freschi* and dates back to medieval times.

Madonna della Salute (Madonna of Health) 21 November

In 1630 the *Signoria* (the Council to the Doge) made a vow to build a church in honour of the Virgin Mary who granted them freedom from the plague. They also promised that the gondolas, which up until the plague had all been painted in bright hues, would remain black from thereafter. (The gondolas during the plague had been painted black and used as funeral conveyances to carry the bereaved and the dead.) A pontoon bridge, as for the Redeemer Day, is built from one side of the Grand Canal on Venice's side across to the Salute island. People pay homage by walking across this bridge to the church and light candles for ill friends or relatives.

Castradina (salted smoked mutton) is traditionally eaten on this day. Originally this meat was supplied by Schiavonia (now Jugoslavia).

All Saints' and All Souls' Days 1 and 2 November

A custom of eating dried beans died out and pastry chefs created tiny little biscuit 'beans' called *'fave'* (broad beans) in blue, red and yellow, which is still the custom today.

San Martino (St Martin's Day)
11 November

San Martino was a nobleman who gave his cloak to a beggar. This saint's day is celebrated mostly by the children, who receive a biscuit cut into the shape of the nobleman and decorated with royal icing, silver balls and chocolates. The other traditional food is a jelly-like quince marmalade which can be cut into any shape and still keep its shape like a biscuit. It is called *persegada* or *cotognata*.

Santa Barbara (St Barbara's Day)
4 December

The Doge on this day traditionally gave all nobles gifts of wild ducks—which abounded in the lagoon beyond Torcello. Soon, though, the number of nobles outnumbered the supply of ducks and the Doge presented his nobles with a small silver coin called *'osela'* (bird). Each Doge, from 1521 onwards for the next 250 years, selected his own subject to decorate these little medallions.

La Vigilia (Christmas Eve)
24 December

The traditional meal eaten on Christmas Eve is eel cooked in whatever way one wishes, although each island does have its own traditional way—usually grilled.

Natale (Christmas Day)
25 December

It is only since the discovery of the Americas that the turkey has started to become traditional—called *gallo d'India* or *dindia* ('Indian cock', literally translated). Veal roast, roasted duck or capon are also traditional.

Capo Danno
(Old Year's Eve and New Year)

There's an old Italian saying which goes 'On New Year wear a new outfit: you'll be well dressed the whole year. You'll eat well too all the year if on Old Year's Eve you prepare many tasty dishes'. The old people advise you to eat chicken and pork, but not at the same meal.

Epifania (Epiphany)
6 January

The *Befana* (old witch) brings all the children who have behaved during the past year a piece of cheese and maybe a present; the naughty children get a piece of coal. This is rock candy coloured yellow and black to resemble cheese and coal.

hare, from a marble cornice, XI century

GLOSSARY

LATIN NAMES

angler fish	*Lophius piscatorius*
clam	*Calcinelloi*
cuttlefish	*Sepia officinalis*
dogfish	*Scyliorhinidae*
goby	*Gobius ophiocephalus*
	Gobius venetorum
mantis prawn (similar to tiger prawn)	*Squilla mantis*
monkfish	*Squatina squatina*
mussel	*Mytilus galloprovincialis*
	Mytilus edulis
pencil bait or razor clam	*Solen capensis*
scampi	*Nephrops norvegicus*
seacat (common octopus)	*Octopus vulgaris*
small (long-finned) squid	*Loligo vulgaris*

UK/US EQUIVALENTS

aubergine	eggplant
castor sugar	sugar, granulated sugar
courgette	zucchini
double cream	heavy cream
fryingpan	skillet
grill	broil
butter beans	(dry) white beans
icing sugar	powered sugar
muslin	cheesecloth
pumpkin	squash
single cream	light cream

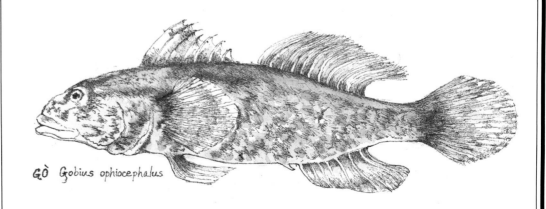

GÒ *Gobius ophiocephalus*

CONVERSION CHARTS

The imperial measures in the recipes and below have been rounded out but this will not affect your results.

It is interesting that measures used in the old Veneto Republic and her colonies were remarkably similar to those we use now: a *libra* was 300 grams, an *oncia* 25 grams, a *dracma* was a pinch, a *scrupolo* 1 gram and a *foglietta* 500 millilitres.

LIQUID MEASURES

millilitres (ml)/litres	cups/ spoons	fluid ounces (fl oz)	
1.5	¼ tspn		
3	½ tspn		
5	1 tspn		
7	1 dssrtspn	¼	
12.5	1 tblspn		
15		½	
25		1	
30		1	
50		1¾	
60	¼ cup	2	
75		2½	
80	⅓ cup	3	
100		3½	
125	½ cup	4	(¼ US pint)
150		5	(¼ UK pint/1 gill)
190	¾ cup	6½	
200		7	
227		8	(½ US pint)
250	1 cup	9	
284		10	(½ UK pint)
300		10½	
455		16	(1 US pint)
500		18	
568		20	(1 UK pint)
750		26	
1 litre		35	
1½ litres		53	

tspn = teaspoon
dssrtspn = dessertspoon
tblspn = tablespoon

SOLID MEASURES

grams (g)	kilograms (kg)	pounds (lb) and ounces (oz)
7		¼oz
15		½oz
20		¾oz
25		1oz
30		1oz
40		1½oz
50		2oz
70		2½oz
75		2½oz
80		3oz
90		3oz
100		3½oz
125		4oz
150		5oz
175		6oz
180		6oz
200		7oz
225		8oz/½lb
250	¼	9oz
300		10½oz
300		11oz
350		12oz/¾lb
370		13oz
400		14oz
454		16oz/1lb
500	½	1lb 2oz
567		1lb 4oz/1¼lb
600		1lb 5oz
650		1lb 7oz
700		1lb 8oz/1½lb
750	¾	1lb 10oz
800		1lb 12oz/1¾lb
900		2lb
1,000	1	2lb 3oz
	1½	3lb 5oz
	2	4lb 7oz

OVEN TEMPERATURES

Heat of Oven	Temperature Range		
	FAHRENHEIT (°F)	CELSIUS (°C)	GAS MARK
Very cool	225–250	110–120	¼–½
Cool	275–300	140–150	1–2
Moderate	325–350	160–180	3–4
Moderately hot	375–400	190–200	5–6
Hot	425–450	220–230	7–8
Very hot	475	240	9

INDEX

Anfora — bas-relief on a 13th century well